T0158874

KEEP THE NEEDLE PEAKING

Gary Corry & Red Neckerson

iUniverse, Inc.
New York   Bloomington

Keep The Needle Peaking

iUniverse books may be ordered through booksellers or by contacting:

iUniverse
1663 Liberty Drive
Bloomington, IN 47403
www.iuniverse.com
1-800-Authors (1-800-288-4677)

ISBN: 978-1-4502-4699-6 (pbk)
ISBN: 978-1-4502-4700-9 (ebk)

Printed in the United States of America

iUniverse rev. date: 8/13/2010

For
Dixie

Foreword

It's amazing how pervasive radio is in our daily lives and how few run it. Mr. Corry has sat in all the seats. There is no better source for the succulent, intimate details than he. Gary has a whale of a tale!

Gary McKee

Introduction

A humorous, entertaining and informative accounting of a fifty year love affair with music radio and a behind the scenes look at the cast of characters who made it happen.

Preface

Disc Jockeys in the 1960s manually cued up and played either 45 rpm single records or 33 1/3 LPs on turntables. After a few dozen plays these vinyl recordings tended to develop irritating scratchy, hissing noise and needed to be replaced with duplicate copies. One of the hazards of the operation was forgetting to adjust speeds of the turntables back to the 45 rpm position or vice versa when going back and forth between album cuts and 45s. Another no-no was to accidently play the wrong side of a 45 or the wrong cut on an LP thereby subjecting the astute listening audience to an unfamiliar rendition of a non-hit song. In the warped minds of radio programmers such mistakes or a few seconds of peaceful silence known by the nefarious title of dead air, would surely cause every single listener to tune out never to return.

Such minor errors caused brief disruptions in the ebb and flow of the station sound and almost always led to a frantic demand from a management type for an explanation. The only answer was totally obvious but a DJ could at least feel confident of having at least one listener.

The introduction of cartridge tapes in the 60s meant that most of the commercials could be recorded and played back much easier than wrestling with reel to reel recorders. For the first few years tape cartridges could only play a little more than 60 seconds of sound without distortion, but as advances were made in the manufacturing process, by the mid-70s most 45 rpm music was being carted up and beamed over the airwaves. Unless a particular LP contained very popular numbers they were still played on turntables. How could such an efficient system be surpassed?

Cartridge tapes had a tendency to break or jam occasionally leading to more hotline calls from Program Directors, Operations Managers, Assistant Managers or someone with an impressive title frantically inquiring as to what had happened.

In the late 80s another great leap sideways saw the introduction of the compact disc. Called CDs in the interest of alphabet letter economy, these small, super-sensitive music delivery systems were touted as being far superior in sound quality to any previous recording device and practically indestructible. This was before it was discovered that a speck of dust or a fingerprint could render them inoperable and someone with decent hearing noticed that the sound reproduction was actually better on the old vinyl LPs. Nevertheless, progress made vinyl records collectors' items.

For a brief period in the late 80s, some stations piddled with a system of small cartridge tapes containing digital audio. Once again, saving radio people from using too many big words, they were known as the DAT system. The little cartridges were expensive and like all tape, theirs became brittle and lost quality as it aged. DAT never really competed with CDs and I presume they ended up in yard sales next to 8 track cartridge tapes so dat's dat.

Today, unless some modern Edison has come out with a new sound reproduction system this morning, radio stations still rely on CDs to an extent and most have the music programmed directly into computers using a program known as Maestro.

While the world outside the radio studios went through the Vietnam war, the struggle for civil rights, the assassinations of Martin Luther King Jr., Jack and Bobby Kennedy, the sexual revolution, the hippy generation, the race to the moon, and ever-changing musical tastes, we meandered from vinyl to cassette, to CD and DAT to music on computer and like the man said, "The hits just keep on coming."

ONE

Start Me Up

A long, long time ago, back before rock and roll music ruined out lives, damaging our psyches beyond repair and leaving us deaf, there was a quiet little community where children could run and play all day with no fear of being subjected to horrors like reality TV shows. Wild fantasies such as television sets, or radio with pictures, would have been considered laughable science fiction as likely as tiny, pocket-sized telephones that one could carry around sending and receiving calls at any time from any location. Pure bad dream material. With no radioactive boob tubes to stare at, people were forced to look at each other and even converse.

"You're ugly."
"Look who's talkin'.".

In a small village such as Rinard, interesting topics were quite limited, so whenever the men loafing in the pool hall or general store grew weary of telling and re-telling the same old dirty jokes, wildly distorted versions of mundane events dominated the conversation.

A friendly greeting or a casual hand wave between a man and woman launched immediate reports that they were engaged in a torrid affair. A wrestling match strictly for fun between two kids was described as an attempted murder. Such exaggerations, twists and blatant falsehoods were perfectly acceptable as the only method available to combat the excruciating boredom of peace and quiet. As we all know, if there is anything a good American hates, its peace and quiet.

During especially dull times such as the dog days of summer when neither human nor animal stirred, even those meager non-events could not be relied upon for conversational material. Thankfully, the miracle of broadcasting, the magical ability of people in far-flung locales to transmit their voices filled the void. Whenever there was a long pause with only an occasional cough or spitting sound emanating from the benches where the local loafers were lounging, one of them would inevitably pipe up with some outlandish statement about something he claimed to have heard on the radio.

"They said on the radio the police raided the Shelton gang's headquarters down at Pond Creek Bottoms and broke up a big bootlegging operation. Shots was exchanged and they was several wounded."

Every story or sentence uttered had to be argued. Failing to do so was a serious insult to the speaker and implied disinterest.

"You're crazy as Hell," someone would say, "Ain't been a bootlegger in 45 miles of there since they allowed 'em to sell liquor and that was 30 years ago."

"You'd ought to know you damn drunk. How many did you say was wounded?"

"Guy on the radio said several. I reckon could'a been a couple or 3 or as many as a dozen. Them Sheltons are always firing away at somebody. If they's nobody else around they go to gunning down one' nuther."

"Yeah, I hate that. We'll sure miss 'em once they're all shot." As a young, innocent boy I noticed that the guy on the radio seemed to hold an important position in life and given my 'druthers I decided early on that I'd druther be a broadcaster than a listener like the town loafers. Okay, so I was just kidding about being innocent.

At the time, I had no idea that I was doing valuable research in preparation for a long career, but I spent a lot of time listening to radio. If I had known where I was headed I could have called it monitoring which sounds much more worthwhile. Baseball games and adventure serials such as The Lone Ranger, Captain Midnight and Superman were my favorites but I would listen to music if I had to.

There was a lot of live programming on the air mainly because recording techniques were rather primitive. If a musician hit a sour note or an actor flubbed his lines, too bad, there were no re-takes. This led to the blooper industry as money-hungry entrepreneurs collected examples of broadcasting screw-ups to sell in books and recordings. A few examples from the so-called Golden Age of Radio include:

Legendary announcer Harry von Zell proclaiming, "The next voice you hear will be that of our new President, Hoobert Heever."

Mel Allen; "It's smipe poking time, gentlemen."

Ralph Edwards; "And here is one of radio's most charming and lovely young sinners."

Weather report: "Tomorrow will be rowdy followed by clain."

These mildly humorous mistakes were considered pretty wild stuff in their day. The word bloopers hadn't come into usage yet and the occasional on-air blunders were called fluffs, a rather effeminate label for a screw-up.

After the advent of wide-spread TV old time radio programming evolved or digressed whichever one prefers, to mostly Disc Jockeys playing music and attempting to entertain, bloopers are deliberately used along with cornball jokes, stunts and obscenities once confined only to pitch-black opium dens and brothels in the slums of Singapore.

We've wandered a long way from the times when The Federal Communications Commission, was going strong and a "damn" or a "Hell" could lead to immediate firing and threats of $25,000 fines, loss of the station's license and a year in federal prison for slinging smut at the tender sensibilities of the listening public. It was a little more costly than say, putting a quarter in the cuss box. Though I had learned to repeat every curse word and obscenity in our fractured English language at an early age, such potentially dire consequences kept me from expressing them over the airwaves.

My first glimpse at the insides of a radio station came on a hot, summer afternoon when another kid and I decided to stop in at WFIW in Fairfield, Illinois after delivering a truck load of wheat to the granary. We had been shoveling the wheat from collecting wagons into the bed of the large truck all day and it was sweaty, back-breaking labor.

Station personnel were congenial and welcomed us in, showed us around and let us observe the broadcaster on duty. A well-dressed man sat in the air-conditioned room calmly sipping coffee while cuing up records, answering an occasional phone call and turning on his microphone to chat briefly between songs. I couldn't help but think how great it would be to trade my job for his.

Turn Me On I'm A Radio

When Top 40 was born in the 50s I was a typical teenage guy, car crazy, girl crazy, restless and impatient to get out of our small, rural community and be somebody. I loved listening to the high-energy, joke-popping, laughing Disc Jockeys who sounded as if they were having a wonderful time playing records.

There were rumors of the big bucks those guys were raking in. I read somewhere that Dick Clark was knocking down a whopping one hundred and seventy five dollars a week as a DJ in Philadelphia before going into TV. I thought if I ever had a job paying that much I'd be rich. That was when gas sold for 35 cents a gallon and Cokes cost a nickel.

St. Louis had three Top 40 stations and some of my favorite personalities were Shad O' Shea and Jack Elliott at KXOK, King Richard and Rex Miller at KWK, and Danny Dark, Dan Ingram, Gary Owens and Ron Lundy on WIL. They were truly all-time greats in the business and St. Louis was home to an incredible wealth of talent.

WLS in Chicago boomed in loud and clear with Rockin' Ron Riley, Dick Biondi, Art Roberts and one poor guy who used the name Dex Card. That was probably a Program Director's idea as I was to learn that they sometimes insist on altering a Jock's name just to make a statement that they are in charge. The majority of programmers were themselves lousy DJs and they have to do something once in a while to justify their existence.

Those classic DJs inspired me to seek a job in radio and over the years I have received many comments and letters from young people telling me that I have motivated them to enter the business. The exciting, fun days of radio are long gone. My advice to anyone contemplating a radio career is, run. Run as fast as you can in the other direction. Sitting all alone in a small control room reading a short positioning statement, meaning inane station slogan, two or three times hourly and programming a computer to play the music would be even more boring than trying to avoid work in a parts warehouse. It wouldn't pay as well either.

After bouncing from one low-paying job to another I entered college at Southern Illinois University with the encouragement of my fiancée Dixie Lee Davis and her parents. I had not decided on a major and in those days young men had a choice of being drafted for two years military service or joining the National Guard or Reserves. I put college on hold to do six months active duty in the Army Reserves, got married and went to work again, still dreaming of being a Disc Jockey in a half serious way.

For the next few years our economic situation improved as I landed a job at the General Motors parts warehouse in St. Louis. It paid well with good benefits but I was bored to tears. Union protocol required us to work as slowly as possible in order to preserve the most jobs. Another guy and I were in charge of a section and we spent most days taking turns playing lookout for the foreman while the other guy hid and napped or read a magazine. I used the time to practice announcing by reading aloud. Quietly.

I took broadcasting correspondence courses and night classes in speech and TV production at Washington University. Finally the lure of broadcasting grew so strong I quit my job and we moved to Carbondale, Illinois where I re-enrolled in college, this time with a Radio/TV major.

The school gave me a student janitorial job and my tuition was paid by the government since I was a military veteran, following my grueling six month tour of duty as a cook's helper at Fort Riley Kansas.

After my first two weeks of pushing a mop I submitted audition tapes to two local radio stations. Our landlord knew the Manager of WRAJ in Anna/Jonesboro, located about twenty miles from Carbondale. He put in a word for me and the manager, Don Michel agreed to give me a trial. The other station manager also called and wanted to hire me.

I was flabbergasted since all I had ever heard from the negative nabobs was how it would be all but impossible for me to get an on-air job in radio. I was far from polished as an announcer and knew nothing about operating the console or board as it is known in the trades, but my measly correspondence courses and speech classes at Washington U. along with my reading aloud practice gave me an advantage over other student applicants whom local stations used as a work force. Being a married man with a child, military experience and more maturity helped too.

The rival station managers argued back and forth for a few days over whose property I was, both pressuring me to commit and I chose WRAJ mainly to avoid offending our landlord and risk losing our nice, little forty dollar a month rental house.

It's Only Rock 'N Roll
And I Kinda' Like Some of It

The radio courses at Southern Illinois University were totally out-dated and the entire department's faculty excepting Doctor Ray Mofield, despised the new Top 40 rage that was sweeping the country in the late fifties and early sixties. Doctor Mofield who had not a single pompous bone in his body, insisted the students just call him Mo. He was a friend to all, ever positive and encouraging to the young hopefuls in his classes. The rest of the radio/TV faculty pretended to dislike him because the head of the department was an old, washed-up grouch who was wont to fly into a slobbering rage at the mere mention of Top 40 radio or rock and roll music.

Learning antiquated network announcing techniques was a laughable waste of time but I played along and made straight A s in my major The first thing I learned at SIU was that only outsiders used the first letter of a station's call letters in conversation. It was 'IL, LS, 'RAJ, unless one wanted to be exposed as a mere listener.

To learn the ropes at WRAJ, er, 'RAJ, I came in everyday during the week to observe the operation. The morning personality Bob Neeley, was a middle-aged man who had show biz experience from his evening job, running the projector at the local drive-in movie theater. He was therefore the station's first hired announcer. Part of his projectionist duties required him to make announcements during intermissions such as specials on hotdogs at the concession stand.

Everyone in town knew and liked Bob. He said the same things at the same times every day. One could best sum up his DJ style with one word; consistency. At seven-ten, it was, "That coffee sure smells good this morning Mother." At seven thirty five it was "School's in session. Slow down and give those kids a brake, b-r-a-k-e." He had a few more just as exciting but you don't really care to read about them.

Bob patiently showed me how to run the console and type the log. I never knew until I got to my next radio job that it is not normal procedure and was most likely an FCC violation to type the official programming log, listing times that all commercials, news, and promos are scheduled after they have aired.

Following a few days of mostly observing Bob Neeley, the boss deemed me ready for my on-air debut. It was to be a leisurely shift featuring "good music" on a Sunday afternoon.

FCC third class license? Check. Straight As in Announcing classes at SIU? Check. Three days of watching Bob Neeley? Check. I was ready. What could possibly go wrong?

Feels Like the First Time

I was alone on the air for the very first time on a beautiful Sunday afternoon in June. It was a day of firsts as I also met my first listener face to face. There wasn't much for me to do except clear the newswire, read newscasts on the hour and half-hour, run the console, take transmitter readings every 30 minutes, type the broadcast log as I went, cue up commercials on an old reel-to-reel tape player, and calmly ad lib for my life while fumbling through a huge pile of beat-up vinyl albums for my next recording. That's all, nothing much. The boss had instructed the raw rookie DJ to play lots of Hawaiian music and Lawrence Welk for his listening pleasure.

The General Manager Don Michel, had graduated college as a music major. Who was I to argue with such credentials? He had told me that he would sit with me during my first solo shift and he did. For about five minutes.

"Do this, push that, read this, type that, and never, never say this or do that." Then he was gone. Gone to take his family on a leisurely Sunday afternoon drive leaving me with a bad case of nerves and a discouraging, "I'll be listening."

Despite feeling like a combination one-man band/ knife juggler I somehow made the station go. There were even brief moments between frantic chore tending that I caught my breath and thought, "I'm on the air. I am a real announcer. A DJ, spinning some of, well, some of the worst records on earth but just think, I'm living the dream, beaming out airwaves over most of the entire county!

That caused a problem. When the boss made his exit he failed to lock the front door. In stalked a large, muscular man about forty years old with an extremely concerned look on his face. Station business I presumed since he stormed directly into the control room.

In a loud voice he demanded to speak to the Station Manager. When I informed him that the Manager was unavailable he demanded to speak to the Chief Engineer. I explained that the Manager, Chief Engineer, sales staff, News Director, Program Director, Production Director and Chief Cook and Bottle Washer were all the same guy, he went into a real rage, demanding that I shut down the transmitter immediately and cease sending those "radio-active, poisonous rays" through his body.

The man appeared to be about one short station ID from violence as I mumbled and stuttered about my lack of knowledge and authority while casting my eyes about for any makeshift weapon heavier than a Don Ho album jacket.

"Turn it off! It's driving me crazy," he yelled. "The station is broadcasting illegally. Don't you feel it? It's running through my entire body day and night. I can't sleep. I can't rest. Do something or I'm going to go out of control."

I decided not to mention that the station signed off every day at sunset. Maybe this is a test, I tried to convince myself. Maybe the boss sent this guy to test my ad-libbing ability in a tight situation. It's not likely, but maybe he wants to see me perform under pressure before really awarding me this minimum wage radio job.

"Tell you what," I said, "I'll turn it way down and call the Manager to come and either fix the transmitter so it will stop sending out those radio-active poisonous rays or just shut the station down."

I turned the studio monitor's volume way down as I spoke and he seemed to believe I had really lowered the power of the broadcast. Poisonous rays? Oh come on. The music can't be that bad.

"Alright, but hurry it up," he proclaimed while turning to leave, "or I'll be back to take care of it myself."

The poor fellow had obviously flipped out completely. Whether due to poisonous rays or listening to the champagne stylings of Lawrence Welk and twangy Hawaiian music was a toss-up.

I hurriedly locked the front door behind him and began dialing and redialing the Boss's unanswered phone number. As I nervously chatted on the air and read the news, the big angry man paced the sidewalk in front of the building, glowering into the window.

I said to myself. "I ain't real sure I'm gonna' like this job."

Working For The Man

Don Michel was a straight-laced, religious sort who censored all records with the slightest hint of sexuality or what he considered indecency. When a fellow announcer broadcasting a football game on a cold evening mentioned that he was wearing his long underwear, Michel called him into his office the next morning and told him if he ever mentioned underwear on the air again he would be fired. I presume the boss was from the old school where undies were considered unmentionables. Why the word unmentionables is mentionable has always been a puzzle to me since it means underwear. I guess that's why he was the General Manager and I was a minimum wage DJ, newsman, play by play announcer and part-time janitor.

Michel was quite proud of his degree in music and he was quick to remind us that he was an authority on all things on key, off key, flat or out of tune. The Ray Conniff Singers had a huge-selling album of Christmas songs that everyone was requesting, but the boss, having noticed that it had been recorded in July in time for mixing, duplication and distribution in December, declared that the singers were flat because they could not have possibly had the Christmas spirit in the summer so the LP was banned from our playlist. Hey Conniff! Here's your lump of coal.

Nearly all of my practical radio education came from Don Michel. He gave me a start in the business and steered me in the right direction. I worked my way through college with the radio job. It wasn't easy being married with a child while carrying a full load in college and working several hours a day for minimum wage. My wife Dixie was a full-time housewife and mother so we scrimped by on my less than huge salary. Fortunately during my three-plus years at WRAJ the federal minimum wage was raised a half-buck an hour two separate times. On both occasions Michel called me into his office, complimented me on my dependability and work ethic, advised me that I should stick to my writing abilities as I would never really make it as an on-air personality, then grandly announced that he had decided to raise my pay. I had to force myself to avoid rolling my eyes and snorting since I was reading the newscasts twice hourly with the lead story being the minimum wage increase.

I had convinced myself that working in commercial radio was my real schooling and instead of having to pay for it as I did at SIU, he was paying me. Not much, but enough to keep a roof over our heads and food on the table. Pass the leftover beans.

When I got the radio job I thought I would be a local celebrity with a following. If that ever happened, it passed unnoticed. Evidently not everyone is as enamored of disc jockeys as I was. Despite the fact that I was being paid at the same rate as the kids serving up burgers at the local drive-in and the old man pumping gas and wiping windshields at the service station, I absolutely loved being on the air.

I really would have worked for nothing if I could have provided for my wife and young son somehow. This was back in the days before cheapskate, penny-pinching management types invented intern programs wherein gullible youngsters are duped into working for nothing under the guise of a learning experience. Well, I'm sure they at least learn to beware of free labor schemes.

The studios were located in the annex of an old hotel building. There was no central air conditioning and in hot weather we remained relatively cool by keeping a window open. Our next door neighbor was a young mortician who had living quarters in his family's funeral home situated just across the alley.

Some evenings when I was segueing album cuts on the FM station he would come over and hang out at the window to chat. Naturally the conversation eventually got around to my inquiring how he could deal with dead bodies and live in the same building housing corpses. He assured me that it was no problem at all, just a way to make a living. Eventually he confessed why he visited me on certain evenings. I found his explanation quite ironic.

"My wife likes to watch scary TV shows, like Twilight Zone. That stuff scares me so bad I can't sleep after I watch it."

We played a few country songs, some of the milder Top 40 hits and a few strange stiffs that the boss selected from the dozens of new records that arrived each week. We also had a lot of local programming such as funeral announcements, hospital admissions and releases, birthdays, and a Classified Column of the Air where for a dollar a holler folks could get a short announcement to sell goats, pot holders, used cars, odd-shaped sweet potatoes and junk that obviously was just on the list because it only cost a dollar for someone to hear his name on the radio.

Following a fifteen minute newscast of such vital information, there was a feature known as the Devotional Hour that lasted forty-five minutes. Michel frowned at my suggestion to rename it the Devotional Three Quarters of An Hour. Local area clergy rotated weekly and spoke from a table in an adjoining studio while the announcer on duty operated the console. Most of the preachers were dignified gentlemen who calmly delivered their messages and thanked us for the air time, but a few real screamers who preached Hell and damnation while staring directly at the low-life sinner running the board, the hedonistic misfit who played that satanic music and told unholy jokes could be a little unnerving.

Another student DJ and I liked to mess with these self-ordained men of the cloth by "accidentally" turning their microphones off at inappropriate times or worse. One weirdo was the Chaplain at the state mental hospital located in the fair village of Anna, and speculation had it that he was also a patient.

He always brought an assortment of religious albums along with cue sheets signaling me when to start the music at various times during his loud, rambling sermons. I would prop my feet up on the console, sip a cup of coffee and completely ignore him while a cohort positioned out of his sight watched him out of the corner of an eye. I pretended to be completely oblivious of him as he glanced ever more nervously to see if I was paying attention leading up to one of his music cues. As he waved frantically, stuttering and blowing his lines I would nudge the turntable's starting switch with my foot and the music would begin to play exactly on cue.

After a few weeks he stopped appearing on the Devotional Hour and his air time was given to another minister. I feel better now. Confession really is good for the soul.

Bob Neeley signed the AM station on the air at the crack of dawn and for a year or so he had a countrified fellow named Frank Perry dropping in each morning at six-thirty to read some of the weird news blurbs that were from the news wire. He would add his own corn pone comments and he became quite popular around town for a while. The cornier the pone, the better they liked him.

Maybe I resented him. Well, yes, I did resent this amateur hick who in my opinion was not nearly as funny as me, a certified announcer. One fine day I exchanged a regular manual typewriter's ink ribbon with one intended for the news machines and typed up a story about a chicken thief by the name of Frank Perry whom the Cape Girardeau police were seeking. I included a description of the suspect that matched Frank down to his floppy, old hat and scruffy boots. I put my story on top of the "kickers" as the odd stories are known in the trade. Cackling fiendishly, I changed the typewriter's ribbon back to the proper one. The CSI Miami crew couldn't have found any evidence to pin on me.

The next morning a visibly shaken Frank was not his usual allegedly funny self on the air. He kept returning to the station every hour on the hour throughout the day checking for follow-ups on the story, mumbling about alibis and mistaken identity. Finally, our lone office employee, a lady by the name of Monika Karraker, either took pity on him or more likely grew sick and tired of him pestering her, and told him it was all a joke. He sighed in relief, grinned and walked out despising me for the rest of his life which is always the result of a good practical joke.

Frank had a habit of repeating his favorite quip about it being "So dark or foggy out that he could barely see over to the Kroger store." This was considered hilarious by Frank and his fans because his sponsor was the rival IGA supermarket. Frank soon lost his sponsor after repeating the line once too often and he was no longer a radio star. I never realized until about twenty-five years later that Frank and the Red Neckerson character had a whole lot in common.

Don Michel was badly wrong about my air work. Although writing is what got me into the major markets and I continued to write for some of the best morning DJs in America including Shad O'Shea, Gary McKee and Rhubarb Jones, and I even had a weekly comedy service for a while, I also garnered excellent ratings as the morning drive Jock in Cincinnati and the New York City markets and did quite well on the air in Atlanta for many years. But enough about me, let's talk about cat feces.

Don Michel did even better. In a stranger than fiction tale, he eventually bought the station from the owner and invested his money in land that happened to contain a certain type of clay which was used to make kitty litter. Michel became a millionaire by selling stuff for cats to go potty on. What path would my career have taken if I had stayed at WRAJ? Don't ask.

TWO

The Sporting Life

Another radio idol of my mine was not a disc jockey but a play by play baseball announcer, Harry Caray, voice of the St. Louis Cardinals. Most remember him as the Chicago Cubs announcer but Harry was with the Cards for twenty-five years and was a beloved part of team as much as any player. He could make the dullest game sound like the final game in the World Series with gross exaggerations of routine plays and his penchant for creating drama where little or none existed. In short, he was the greatest play by play announcer of all time as a young man. I wanted to be like him.

While majoring in Radio/TV in college, the school's radio station, WSIU-FM broadcast the football, basketball and baseball games utilizing the raw talents of students taking a class in sportscasting, much to the chagrin and often downright rage of Saluki fans.

Baseball games were rarely aired but I was assigned along with a fellow classmate to call the play by play of a home game. Everything went just swimmingly for our pre-game show and at the scheduled starting time we happily awaited the umpires call to "Play ball!"

Unfortunately, there had been a nice rain shower that morning and the field was deemed too wet to play on, but with a little landscaping by the ground crew and the sunshine, the game would begin sooner or later. Back at the studio an idiot was pulling a shift running the board and had no idea what to do.

The log said baseball game and he was not about to violate the format. The other kid and I ad-libbed for an hour and a half before the game started. To this day I'm not sure how we managed to find the material to fill the time. We gave very detailed descriptions of guys raking the base-paths, putting down sand, wielding shovels and playing catch. It had to be the worst so-called sportscast in history up until perhaps beach volleyball.

I knew from that day forth that I would never have a problem filling a few minutes with the spoken word. According to a few Program Directors I should have learned to be silent.

Meanwhile, back at WRAJ I was soon promoted with no increase in pay to play by play announcer for the Anna-Jonesboro High School football and basketball games. It wasn't long before I decided that I did not want to be the next Harry Caray after all.

Are You Ready For Some Mudball?

As far as I am concerned there are only two seasons in a year, football season and those other seven months when life is barely worth living. The only times in my life that I didn't enjoy football was when I played or broadcast the games. I went out for football as a five foot, four inch, one hundred twenty pound freshman and soon noticed that when I wasn't being beaten to a pulp by bigger, older players, I was either on the verge of a heat stroke or frostbite as the brutal practices began in July's stifling heat and finally ended in the dead of winter. Until my junior year I never played a down in a real game, which was probably a good decision by the coaches.

My advice: Enjoy football by watching someone else's misery. Just sit down and relax. I didn't get into sports play by play because I was a frustrated athlete. No, in addition to playing records, reporting the news twice hourly, typing the broadcast logs, taking transmitter readings, mouthing live commercials and clearing the teletype machines and reading two newscasts every hour, my minimum wage pay at WRAJ required me to broadcast the local high school games. I would load the equipment into my old car and head out alone, my engineer, spotter, color man and sideline reporter only figments of my imagination.

My most memorable nightmare, I mean sportscasting experience, was the game during a driving rain storm with the players numbers totally obliterated by mud as I strained to see the action from my lousy position in one end zone. The host team was not overly cordial to the visiting team's play-by-play star so they ordered me to set up out of everyone's way.

I just made up plays and threw in random names from the rosters, faking about ninety percent of the game. I was sure that I would be fired the next day, but the boss told me that my work was definitely improving. The only negative reviews I received were from the usual source, parents whining that I didn't praise their kids enough. I wonder if John Madden ever had to go through such debacles.

More advice: Leave the play-by-play to others. Just sit down, watch the game and make comments as you wish. There is no pressure, and you won't be fined or fired for cussing. Some claim that you don't have to drink beer and eat a lot of junk food to enjoy the game, but I am convinced that it helps.

In fact, it is the only thing enjoyable when your team is getting refereed into yet another humiliating loss.

We were taught certain basic guidelines in sportscasting class, thus I have not been able to enjoy a game on radio or TV for decades as runny-mouthed morons on most broadcasts violate every rule in the book. During a telecast we were ordered to shut up and provide a minimum of chatter since viewers could see for themselves what was happening.

My old professors must be spinning in their graves even though almost all of them were teaching because they failed as broadcasters. "Teams" of ex-players, color men and second guessing, name dropping, nostalgia whining comedians crowd the booths ruining the games with distracting claptrap. I give thanks before each game as a way of saying Grace for the mute button.

The most challenging game to call is baseball due to the slow pace and redundancy. The easiest is basketball due to the non-stop action and football is somewhere in between. Those are the only real sports no matter what someone tries to tell you. Anything else such as soccer, volleyball, golf or poker are shams that only dumb people watch not realizing they are aired only to avoid another sleazy reality show.

My most vivid memory of an SIU Saluki basketball broadcast I took part in is actually a post-game event. The game was aired on a network of five stations and I was thrilled to be one of the announcers of such a prestigious event. Even better, one station taped the game and played it back an hour later so I was able to listen to myself on my car radio as I drove home. I stopped for gas at a service station, one of those now long gone places where a real human came out and pumped the gas into your tank.

"Hey, that's me," I said to the bored looking attendant as I turned up the volume. He frowned, hurriedly finished with his chores, grabbed my money and stalked back inside, obviously taking me for a complete nut. I guess he was unfamiliar with delayed broadcasts.

I'm Outta' Here Anna, You Too Jonesboro

After three years at WRAJ and WSIU-FM I had not only learned everything there was to know about radio, I was beginning to forget a few things, so I decided it was well past time to move on. In reality, I knew that I was destined to work for minimum wage until I received a raise with my first Social Security check unless I advanced to a larger market. In the fall of '63 I started sending out audition tapes in reply to Help Wanted ads in Broadcasting magazine.

It was déjà vu all over again as I received offers from two stations. One from WIBV, Belleville, Illinois, a powerful, full-time, so-called adult music station, and another from WTCJ in tiny Tell City, Indiana. The choice was obvious. I could take the job in the large St. Louis market or in another small, rural community. Admittedly, the Program Director at 'TCJ was much more eager to hire me. In fact, he broke down and cried into the phone when I turned down his offer. I firmly believe I avoided working for a seriously unstable person. Frankly, my audition tapes were not that good.

Don Michel was visibly angry when I gave notice. He warned me that I was making a mistake by leaving my minimum wage job and that I would regret it. So far I haven't. I had been a loyal employee for over three years as other college student DJ wannabees came and went. Most of them were starry-eyed dreamers who mistakenly thought they were good enough to grab a major market job with a big salary but in reality few had any work ethic or were willing to donate the time and effort to succeed. I needed the income for my family. I honed my announcing and writing skills at WRAJ but it was past time to hand the headphones to the next rookie.

No one cried when I left WIBV and I was only approved to fill the seven-to-midnight slot with hesitation by station owner/management. The beleaguered Program Director, Lee Coffee had been searching for a suitable hire for months but each prospect was rejected by the big brass. He was elated when they finally agreed to give me a shot. I was just as happy as he was, jumping directly from the boondocks to a suburban major market station that garnered good ratings in the metropolitan area. I had a lot of relatives in St. Louis and my great aunt Laura owned a boarding house where I could stay until my wife Dixie and our son Russ could join me in our own place. I had a good paying job on a successful station in a familiar city. What could possibly go wrong?

THREE

Hello, Goodbye

What went wrong at WIBV was another first show nightmare. This time it was not an enraged critic that barged in from off the street. The addled soul was me. Everything was going fine and dandy as I played album cuts, read five minute newscasts on the hour and smugly enjoyed the feeling of having tens of thousands of listeners.

About nine o'clock I received a phone call from my wife that led to the end of my extremely brief WIBV tenure. She excitedly told me that a man by the name of Bob Keith Gordon had called and wanted to hire me for a writing job at WCPO, Cincinnati. He wanted me to call him immediately. I had been wrong. It was not two stations wanting to hire me at the same time as had happened when I took my first job. It was three. I told Dixie I would give Bob Keith a courtesy call, but there was no way I would quit my gig at WIBV right after starting.

I called Bob while on the air, keeping the needle peaking as we say in radio, or maybe it's just me and was instantly won over by his enthusiastic sense of humor and his appreciation for my talents. The offer to practically double the WIBV salary helped too.

I had sent a ridiculous gag resume in reply to a blind ad seeking a writer/ part time DJ for a major market station. Tired of being ignored by stations where I had sent resumes detailing how experienced, reliable and wonderful I was, I typed up a couple of pages describing myself as a no-good, hopeless, lazy, drunken bum intermingled with sarcastic one-line jokes. Bob was roaring with laughter and decided that I was exactly who he wanted to write bits for the morning DJ and funny promos for the station.

Bob had been the Program Director at "Fun Radio," WFUN, Miami and WCPO management wanted him to bring that format to Cincinnati. I accepted his offer and started fretting about informing WIBV.

In those days I was a smoker and if I ever needed a cigarette to calm my nerves it was after I hung up the phone with Bob Keith and started feeling terrible about having to inform the nice Program Director who had fought to give me a job in a big market that I was bailing out after one lousy shift.

I was to read a five minute newscast at eleven fifty-five then a sign-off announcement as WIBV went dark at midnight. I gathered my news copy and put an album cut on the air. Luckily it just happened to be the first cut on a Jackie Gleason's Orchestra LP. It's no wonder I recall the very record to this day. I ducked out to have a quick smoke, quite distracted, worrying about how I would break the news the next morning. Since it was my first evening on the job, I hadn't received a door key as yet, but I figured I could just prop the door open with the sturdy latch. I no sooner stepped outside when I heard the most sickening, frightening sound imaginable, a "click" as the door shut, locking me out. It was an unbelievably stupid trick that causes me to mutter in disgust and shame decades later. There was nary a soul to help me. I was alone outside the station building located on a lonely stretch of highway miles from town. My luck was not totally down the toilet as I had my car keys in a pocket. I jumped into the driver's seat and sped down the road searching for a phone. The radio beamed out the lovely orchestral melody, "Moon over Miami." It never entered my flummoxed mind at the time, but perhaps some sarcastic astral spirit was ribbing me for double-crossing the WIBV Program Director and accepting a job from a guy calling from…where else? Miami.

I spotted the neon lights of a small tavern and roared into the parking lot, ran in and breathlessly asked if they had a pay phone. Before cell phones ruined life as we knew it, every establishment had a pay phone. Folks often carried pocket change too, an ancient ritual that passed into history with the advent of credit cards. By some miracle I had Lee Coffee's phone number and coins for the pay phone.

I dialed the number and listened nervously as it rang repeatedly, silently praying that Jackie Gleason and the gang would keep the needle peaking until I figured a way to get back into the studio. Finally Lee picked up and sleepily told me to call the engineer who was on duty at the transmitter. I never realized there was an engineer at the transmitter but it explained why I didn't need a First Class FCC license. Obviously the Program Director had not been listening to my great show as I thought, but enjoying a nice sleep.

I rushed out of the joint after giving the engineer a rapid call, leaving the few barflies scratching their heads, wondering what the nervous character making frantic phone calls was up to. The engineer drove from the transmitter building and we arrived at the station at the same time. He calmly unlocked the door and I rushed in just as the last notes on the album faded into silence. I panted my way through the newscast and read the sign-off announcement. I drove to Aunt Laura's to spend a restless night, dreading the dawn like a man facing the gallows.

The next day I entered the Program Director's office apologizing profusely for being such an idiot and causing the sign-off time to be about five minutes late.

"No big deal," he said. "We have a full-time license. It doesn't matter what time we sign off. You did well. I'll get you a key today. Sorry I forgot it yesterday. Let's go over just a couple of things." I was feeling worse with each passing moment. He was such a perfect gentleman, seemingly unconcerned with my boneheaded blunder.

"I need to tell you something," I said, and quickly explained about sending out other audition material and the job offer from Cincinnati. He was quite disappointed, mentioning how long it had taken the owners to approve an evening DJ but said, "I don't blame you. I can't fight that kind of money." The money I was offered to go to WUBE would be laughable today, but inflation does weird things to the economy. I gave him two weeks' notice like any reputable soul should do and he informed me that it would be okay to leave at the end of the week. My luck. Lee Coffee was one of the nicest guys in the history of the radio business and I got to work for him five days.

The owner/managers in the big office weren't as forgiving. When tax return time rolled around a few months later I dutifully wrote requesting a W-2 form and got back a terse reply stating that Gary R. Corry had never been employed by WIBV. Gee fellows that's not going to help my resume. Why not add, "Never heard of him, he never darkened our door, he never once even listened to the station and if he ever does we will beat him to a bloody pulp."

WIBV later sold out to Disney and the station was moved into St. Louis with new call letters. An FM station in Marion, Illinois picked up the old call letters and is now WIBV-FM. I can't imagine why. I presume WIBV stood for "We're in Belleville." Maybe some sentimental type left the station and took the call letters with him.

This Time Tomorrow,
Reckon Where I'll Be?

I checked out the WCPO studio setup the evening prior to my scheduled arrival. I was determined to avoid yet another first day calamity. The radio station was located at the end of a steep, winding driveway atop a hill in a building housing a TV station. It was a twenty-four hour a day operation. No danger of locking myself out. There was a security guard on duty. No danger of a deranged listener barging into the studio. This time, I was convinced that nothing could go wrong.

The Assistant General Manager of WCPO AM/FM and Channel 9, WCPO TV was a straight-laced, ultra-conservative ex-FBI agent by the name of Bob Gordon. The new Program Director had the same name so he was forced to call himself Bob Keith. He made me feel welcome, and a valuable member of the team, complimenting me profusely on my creative writing skills.

Bob was a classy gentleman who always did a positive, upbeat show. I will forever appreciate the opportunity he gave me to jump to a major market, Top 40 station and for his support. I was a green, 20- something coming from a tiny market and suddenly these experienced major market veterans were laughing and complimenting me on my writing while accepting me as a friend and equal member of the team. I could not have been much happier.

Our work was certainly cut out for us. WCPO at one time had been the Top 40 leader in town. Then WSAI came along with a much better signal and took over the number one ranking. WCPO went through a series of format changes rather unsuccessfully and one strange day Bob Gordon arrived at the stations wearing a ten gallon hat and cowboy boots, waving a guitar and loudly announcing his brilliant idea for a new direction in radio; full-time Hootenanny! A wonderful example of why management should stay out of programming. Way, way out.

In case you weren't around at the time or have blissfully forgotten, America was swept up in a folk music craze in the early 60's. Such artists and groups as The Kingston Trio, The Brothers Four, Peter, Paul and Mary, Joan Baez, Bob Dylan and a myriad of others twanged about peace, love and flower power. There were TV shows featuring folk music. The most popular one was called Hootenanny, a term for folk singing festivals. I think they were originally intended to obtain information from enemy combatants prior to the invention of water boarding.

While the new, Fun Radio staff gathered, writing, recording and preparing for the Top 40 debut, we had to listen to the caterwauling, twanging sounds of Hootenanny Radio for several days. It was quite obvious why the format failed. It did not wear well. The format lasted six weeks, which was far too long.

I was happy to be writing for one of my radio idols, Shad O' Shea, whom I had enjoyed listening to when he was at KXOK in St. Louis. Shad possessed a sarcastic wit and as a former speech therapist he could perform many hilarious character voices. He was a six foot six tower of talent who also wrote books and composed songs. He was teamed with Mike Gavin after a few months at WCPO and the two were a great combination. Mike was generally the straight man for Shad or one of his characters and he added a warm sense of stability to the show. There was no jealousy or resentment between them which is generally present in team shows, and they remained close friends for life.

Other members of the on-air staff for Fun Radio were the Program Director Bob Keith, Dick Provost, Miles Foland, Rock Robins and Jack McCoy. My duties were to write humorous jokes or routines for the morning show and to make every promo or station related announcement funny, creative and unique. I was also required to write commercial copy for the sales department, a duty I shared with a young guy named Rick Blackburn.

Rick was the copy writer and fill-in DJ prior to my arrival. Despite his being assured that his job was secure, in a few short weeks he was terminated. He could write suitable commercial copy but he did not have a flair for comedy and his on-air work was unremarkable. I felt for him as we had become friends, but I must admit to being thrilled to go on the air part-time. There was no need for a pity party. Rick went into record promotion and found his mission in life. From a local representative he rocketed to the top job at CBS records in just a few years. Getting fired from a crummy job is always a blessing and a window of opportunity.

The business can turn a person into a cold-hearted human being, reluctant to form friendships or permanent relationships. No sooner does one become acquainted with a co worker until one of the two is fired or decides to leave.

Management had authorized a budget of $200,000 for the promotion of WCPO Fun Radio, an unbelievable amount of dough in the early 60's. They obviously expected a quick return on their investment which of course put enormous pressure on the radio staff.

Helicopters buzzed The Queen City dropping hundreds of thousands of fliers with coded numbers good for huge prizes consisting of cash, fur coats, appliances and new cars. Just listen to 1230, WCPO Fun Radio and call in when your number is announced! With billboards, TV spots and unheard of giveaways to launch our new format, what could possibly go wrong?

FOUR

And We'll Have Fun, Fun, Fun 'Til ...

Fun Radio hit the airwaves on Monday, September 17, 1963. Despite a few, well okay, despite several rough spots and challenges, we were the talk of the town and the phones were being blown out, overloaded with calls from people as ravenous as slobbering hyenas, eager to grab some of the contest loot.

One of the first lessons I learned about major market radio was how contests work. Contests are on the air for three different purposes. Small prizes such as a couple of sandwiches, a lube job, or a pair of tickets to a boring trade show are something the sales department threw in to give a client free on-air plugs. Program Directors spend a lot of time trying to keep such distracting clutter off the air.

Another contest may award t-shirts, caps, coffee mugs or other small trinkets that are adorned with the station logo. These prizes are to promote the station, though after giving away literally thousands of caps and t-shirts a DJ has a better chance of spotting an albino baboon in a leisure suit than a person wearing one of the caps or t-shirts in public.

No one expects small prize contests to cause a surge in the ratings. Hyping the book as it is sometimes called, requires either big money or big money items. Stations spend enormous amounts of money during rating periods in an effort to get new listeners at least temporarily, so as to create the false impression that all these greedy contestants are loyal fans. If the contest works, the new numbers are presented to advertising agencies and prospective time buyers as gospel proof of how many people can be reached by advertising on the station.

Everyone knows how big contests skew the numbers but it's easy for programmers and management to claim the ratings increases come from their brilliant guidance and for on-air personnel to convince themselves it is due to their fabulous talents.

There is a certain breed of primates who seemingly exist solely to enter radio station contests. They call constantly all day and all night, attempting to be the one who is selected to vie for the prize. Some of the folk are tuned in to many different stations simultaneously and have several separate phones at their disposal. They are known to counterfeit so-called lucky number tickets, or crudely alter numbers on an entry form.

A part time DJ who was formerly a notorious contest participant would enter other station's call-in games even while on the air. He had notes of times they asked for calls and once won a prize on a station in Los Angeles while working the all-night shift in Atlanta. He also won the grand prize of a brand new Jaguar with the lucky key, much to the chagrin of a rival station.

Disc Jockeys may receive phone calls from females inviting them to drop by for an intimate chat about how badly they need the cash prize and what they would do to win it. I doubt if this news comes as a shock, but big money contests bring out the worst in people.

Management decreed that we would further promote the new 'CPO with a one-hour TV special on Channel 9. I was assigned the chore of scripting several comedy routines to be interspersed into the show which was primarily a dance party with the DJs hosting students from a local high school. Basically, my script called for the Jocks to be hit in their faces with cream pies every time one of them tried to make a sincere pitch plugging the station. Trust me, it was hokey but irreverently funny.

Sets were constructed, the teens arrived all dressed up and groomed as if ready to attend a semiformal dance, the DJs performed well, the pies flew and the Fun Radio TV special was in the can. When the TV crew began the editing process they discovered that the audio was distorted, making the entire taped show worthless. I hope to this day the audio was not messed up by an errant cream pie. The furious GM ordered the tape erased and the project was scrapped. Could things get any worse? Oh yeah.

I was in the continuity/traffic/sales office with a group of co-workers when someone shouted that President John Kennedy had been shot. We rushed to the lobby where a Channel 9 CBS TV monitor ran constantly and the terrible news was confirmed. Along with every other radio station we immediately switched programming to full-time news coverage of President Kennedy's assassination.

For the next several days we carried CBS radio news and played somber instrumental or religious music between newscasts. The initial momentum from the new format launch was completely erased. It would be difficult to imagine a more tragic beginning for a format calling itself Fun Radio.

Days later, following the President's funeral, we attempted to resume Top 40 programming. We were under orders from the Big Cheese department to use a subdued approach. No joking around or disrespectful music would be allowed until they declared that a proper mourning period had passed. Some fun.

WCPO radio studios, if a tiny, cramped corner of the building can be called that, consisted of one medium-sized room where the sales staff and

Secretary, Continuity Writers and the lady who typed the program logs, know in broadcasting as the Traffic Department, elbowed one another fighting for access to a few typewriters and phones. It was not an atmosphere conducive to deep concentration and creative writing. The Sales Manager had a small adjoining office and the Program Director's office was located in the walkway to the on-air and production studios. There was more much privacy in the men's room. One of the stalls might have felt roomier too.

The on-air studio was a claustrophobic area approximately six feet wide by twelve feet long. There was barely room for the console and a chair. News room? We don't need no stinkin' news room! The WCPO call letters stood for Cincinnati Post, the Scripps Howard newspaper. Unbelievably, the radio news staff was located miles from the station in the newspaper offices downtown. The theory was that they would be right on top of all the late-breaking stories with access to dozens of reporters. There is nothing like having a bunch of hard-drinking neer-do-wells with whom to swap dirty jokes.

Since the station's signal could not be picked up in the newspaper building, at scheduled times for news, we could only play the recorded intro and hope the reporter was alert and prepared to go on air. Sometimes they were. At other times, the "bright and tight" Top 40 format became several long moments of dead air followed by the loud clicking sound of a microphone being turned on, then a breathless announcer gasping and sputtering through a few minutes of so-called news.

The morning team, Shad and Mike, ever creative and funny, recorded their own news intro consisting of a make-believe chair situated on a hydraulic lift. At news time, they would crank it up in full sound and the chair would supposedly rise, creaking and groaning to a great height, then one of them would shout, "Okay, it's ready, drop him in it," and the unsuspecting news reporter, ensconced in the newspaper office miles away would read the report totally unaware of being part of a comedy routine. The usual, dour, faux authoritative delivery was what made the bit hilarious.

Most members of the news department were solid professionals. The guy who was usually relating details of current events from his imaginary perch on the Shad and Mike Show was a rather pompous character who had a bad habit of burping and belching after every few lines. Not loudly, but enough to be extremely annoying to a careful listener. He dropped by the station to pick up his paycheck and boast about an upcoming trip to New York City where he was to audition for a job with the CBS Television Network. Everyone had a good chuckle at his expense as we all agreed that he was by far the weakest link in the WCPO news crew.

A few days later he returned smugger than ever. He said that after auditioning on camera at CBS and receiving the standard, "We'll keep your tape on file and let you know, blah blah," he moseyed across the street to ABC TV, auditioned for them and was hired. We thought he was lying but obviously he was able to control his belching and soon afterward there he was, reporting for ABC Television as their West Coast correspondent. Good for him. I love a success story, but I could never watch him on TV without picturing him precariously clinging to the armrests of a chair on the end of a pole thirty feet in the air while belching.

Our cramped AM facility was approximately half the size of the WRAJ studios back in little Anna-Jonesboro, Illinois. I had imagined luxurious digs worthy of a major market station. I've always had a wild imagination.

We could have been considered the red-headed step child of uncertain parentage in the building but for WCPO FM. That consisted of a lone bank of reel to reel tape players broadcasting elevator music. The few announcements were recorded in advance and station engineers changed from one reel of sleep-inducing music to the next every few hours, but only if they remembered to do so. It was not uncommon that no one noticed WCPO FM was off the air until one of the extremely rare listeners phoned in a wakeup call.

The union engineers were a group of laid-back, conservative, middle-aged gents who were not especially fond of the new fangled, obnoxious rock and roll which had shoved aside their beloved big band sounds and even the semi-beloved, short lived Hootenanny format. Since it was a union station, we could not touch the recording equipment without the assistance of an authorized, dues paying engineer. This was another of those rough spots I mentioned. They had little concept of Top 40 production or a sense of humor. It was less than encouraging seeing a recording engineer shake his head in disgust as one of the jocks mouthed the words of one of my hilarious scripts. Talk about a tough room. These dudes hadn't laughed since Hollywood ruined movies for them by adding sound.

The Chief Engineer, struggling with a radio-related technical problem was heard to mutter his motto, "Man was not meant to transmit his voice." He seemed to believe he was quoting scripture.

Bob Keith's microphone failed in the midst of his show and he frantically rang the hotline number in the engineering office located at the far end of the building. When he explained his problem was trying to do a radio show without a microphone, the Chief inquired, "How soon do you need it?"

A DJ hero of mine is the guy in California who grew frustrated with a malfunctioning tape cartridge machine that the engineers kept ignoring. He ad libbed a little contest and gave it away to the fourth caller.

FIVE

Hey, Mister DJ

Disc Jockeys did not have the best of reputations in the early days of rock and roll and Top 40 radio. Many older folks despised the new music, dismissing it as a passing fad that would soon burn itself out and then "good" music would return to the airwaves. TV hosts sneered while using rock music as the butt of vicious humor.

The term rock and roll was used quite loosely, covering everything from Elvis and The Beatles, to soft ballads by Brenda Lee or Andy Williams. If it was a hit, the oldsters didn't like it and that was that. They also despised the dregs of society who played such mind numbing rubbish on the air.

Even within the station DJs are often resented. Three hours was the standard on-air work day for Jocks while office workers put in their eight hours for much less pay. Being alone in the studio is a lonely job and when a shift ends the DJ may have a desire to talk to someone face to face only to be met with frowns and insults from behind the scenes toilers. As Hall of Fame DJ Gary McKee once said, "The Disc Jockeys hate the sales people, the sales people hate the DJs and everybody hates me."

A fact that management and time sellers often forget while basking in their executive vanity, that to the hundreds of thousands of listeners the radio station is the voices they hear on the air and no one else. If a part-time, minimum wage, teenage intern is on the air pulling a weekend shift that is the radio station, not the titled upper management type over at the country club.

As if pretentious management types aren't bad enough, often their wives become critics and programming experts who order their intimidated husbands to remove certain records or to fire a DJ because she was embarrassed by a remark someone made about the station at a social gathering. A common trait among whip-cracking executives in the workplace is how they are hen-pecked wimps at home.

Cincinnati, being a very conservative city, was especially slow to accept changing musical tastes. I witnessed several top acts that were selling out from coast to coast perform in less than half-full venues. Thanks to some of the fly-by-night, immoral Jocks who certainly deserved their disreputable images, I was reluctant to reveal my occupation to strangers.

Admitting one was a Rock Jock could elicit a sneer and an accusation of playing dirty, un-American, hippie music and poisoning the minds of children. It was not exactly the star reception I had once expected. I noticed that as a rule, the less talented a DJ happened to be, the bigger his ego. I could have made a pretty penny selling those characters T-shirts with the slogan, "Ask me about me."

Some unyielding, power-crazed Program Directors would fire a Jock for the slightest infraction or format violation, real or imagined. A couple seconds of dead air, uttering a word over the inane lyrics of an imbecilic song, or just because he was your boss and he decided you didn't sound happy and positive enough were all grounds for dismissal, and some folks wonder why DJs are paranoid and insecure.

The outside world, even as close as the in-station office personnel never understood how a few measly hours playing records and talking could wear a person out physically and mentally. It is hours of constant stress and tension, timing everything to the second while forcing oneself to sound bright and cheerful even while experiencing sickness or personal problems. A DJ is only as good as his last record intro. When I went in to do my show I double-parked and left the motor running.

The British Are Coming, Armed With Guitars!

During the Fun Radio period the British invaded, led by The Beatles. American teens went totally berserk over what the media liked to redundantly call the mop-topped quartet. I loved The Beatles and still do but their fame also opened the floodgates for any artist or group with a British accent. Some of them like the Rolling Stones actually had talent and staying power. Others, Freddie and the Dreamers, Wayne Fontana and the Mindbenders, Herman's Hermits, The Troggs, Ian Whitcomb, well, you be the judge. Feel free to judge harshly.

Shad O' Shea, a music composer and producer on the side, despised Beatlemania and the latest British Invasion. If it had been up to him we would have recruited Minute Men to shoot the English intruders and dump their records into the Ohio River as an update to the Boston Tea Party. Shad thought we should support American artists first, meaning the ones he managed.

A Hard Day's Night

For once, the town's concert boy-cotters fought for tickets when The Beatles appeared at the Cincinnati Gardens, unfortunately for us, sponsored by WSAI. Programming whiz, Rex Jones came up with a scheme to capitalize on the monumental event. He had thousands of fliers printed stating that WCPO welcomed The Beatles, hoped everyone enjoyed the concert and invited them to tune in tomorrow to 1230 to win Beatles albums.

We Disc Jockeys were to stand outside the venue passing out these fliers to giddy Beatlemaniacs. Shad, Mike, Bob Keith and I tried it for a while. The kids cursed us, spat on us, wadded up the papers and threw them back at us, fully aware that WSAI was the station responsible for bringing their beloved moptops to town and that we were trying to claim credit. They frequently accused us of being WSAI copycats, forgetting that WCPO was the original Top 40 station before some brilliant management type decided such a format was too radical for Cincinnati. Good point.

After a few minutes of abuse we wisely dumped several thousand fliers into trashcans and headed for the nearest bar to console ourselves. I was due back at the station in a few hours to work the overnight shift so I limited myself to a couple of beers. Bob decided to hit the tequila and before long and without too much effort he talked me into trying my first margarita. Not bad, I thought, a little bitter, but, not bad. Mike warned that tequila was a drink that could sneak up on you and leave you drunk before you know it. Big deal, I can handle my liquor.

Suddenly the room began to spin and I lost track of whatever blather we were exchanging. I recall almost vomiting when someone mentioned that it was a tradition to polish off the tequila then eat a worm that was in the bottle. I have never had a drop of tequila since the evening of The Beatles concert in 1964.

Another Tequila Sunrise

The guys dropped me off at the station and somehow I managed to live through the next six hours, playing what we were calling the King 30 hits in The Queen City, introducing records then resting my dizzy head on the console between songs. The night was over in about six weeks as the queasy feeling evolved into a splitting headache. It was one of those nights I was glad to have only a few listeners, none of them in station management.

I have pulled many a shift with a bad cold, the flu, right after having two wisdom teeth pulled and countless times without sleep in the previous twenty-four hours but they were all downright fun compared to my tequila sunrise adventure. For a few years afterward I even got a slight twinge of nausea whenever I heard a Beatles song.

Disc Jockeys who came and went were known as Job Hoppers, moving from station to station one jump ahead of jealous husbands, irate fathers, bill collectors or the sheriff. Not helping stability, many stations were labeled Swinging Doors for their habit of constant hiring and firing. Just as some DJs started sending out audition tapes as soon as they landed one gig, some programmers kept Help Wanted ads running in trade publications on a permanent basis. As the saying went, you could tell how much a DJ was worth by the size of his U Haul trailer.

Disc Jockeys can possess enormous egos while being quite paranoid and insecure at the same time. This holds true for any facet of show business where one is only as good as his last performance. Wearing a set of headphones and hearing your own voice, amplified and often with a touch of reverb, knowing that you are speaking to thousands of listeners can give a person a certain rush and a feeling of power that is addictive. It is a feeling that cannot be accurately described and has to be experienced. I loved it and never felt more alive than when I was on the air. I could not understand a DJ who would complain about working a long shift or even an extra hour. I wanted all the air time I could get. As someone said, "Success is not the key to happiness. Happiness is the key to success. If you love what you are doing you will be successful."

It comes as no big revelation, but Disc Jockeys are regular human beings, some flighty and weird while others are wonderful men and women. A large percentage of those I have worked with are kindred souls and lifelong friends whom I hold in high respect. A radio career is a life of insecurities and can lead to a dead end with few or no lasting benefits, but it's either the life we chose or it chose us.

I believe that there are no coincidences and there is a reason for every person we meet. Everyone I meet and interact with along the way makes an impression on me as I do on them. I can only hope that most of the impressions I leave are positive.

Can You Hear The Music?

In real estate its location, location, location. In AM radio its signal, signal, signal. A lot of talented WCPO Disc Jockeys came and went from 1963-1965 and the station programming was quite good. It really doesn't matter how good you are if they can't hear you. Beaming out a puny 1,000 watts in the daytime and a pathetic 250 at night it was miraculous that we even competed in a tough radio market.

Our direct competition WSAI had a strong signal with 5,000 watts full time. WLW was a clear channel 50,000 watt flame thrower with excellent DJs including Richard King, one of the most clever radio personalities I have ever heard. WKRC was number one in the market with great entertainers including Jerry Thomas, an incredibly gifted DJ. WCKY, another 50,000 watt station was nothing to take lightly.

Manning the turntables from midnight to six AM had some advantages. Though I may have had more listeners on the 500 watt WRAJ back in little Anna-Jonesboro than I had at 3 AM on WCPO and knew all my listeners names, addresses and social security numbers, I could violate the format or make up my own, saying and doing anything I pleased.

Meanwhile everyone ignored the potential of the powerful WCPO FM signal. FM radio was not to explode onto the scene until the great Top 40 genius Bill Drake had the nerve to put the format on the air with WOR-FM in New York City. Radio programmers then as now, following their timid monkey-see, monkey-do instincts were jarred from their stupor and before long FM ruled to the point of practically destroying AM properties. Switchy switchy. From being near worthless while AM was wonderful, FM frequencies now rule and AM stations, unless 50,000 watt powerhouses are struggling to survive.

WCPO management would never give a Program Director much more time than they allowed for the disastrous Hootenanny debacle. Ratings were taken weekly by phone calls under the Hooper system and though we actually got better numbers than our pathetic market coverage would indicate, heads would roll and a new PD would be named if we didn't overtake strongly entrenched WSAI in a matter of weeks. Bob Keith was demoted to midday

DJ and a fellow by the name of Rex Jones was given a trial. At the time I was working 9 to 5 as a copy writer and temporarily pulling the all night shift as Jack McCoy had been fired. I slept from about 7 to 8, A M and another few hours in the evening. I felt like the baker in the old Dunkin' Donuts commercial, no sooner asleep than roused out of bed and back at it.

Rex loved to party a little too much too often and soon he was gone. Management brought in a Program Director on a glowing reference from the departing Jones whose name I will not reveal simply because it is another common radio name. Who knows, one or two of them may be decent workers.

When this move proved to be a disaster ratings-wise, Rex Jones called back snickering that his recommendation was a prank that he pulled for revenge. His successor was the laziest person ever to venture into a radio station. He was perpetually late if he showed up at all for his nine to noon air shift.

An unfortunate concert promoter had booked The Beach Boys at the height of their popularity for a Cincinnati Gardens concert and by some miraculous coup, WCPO was chosen over WSAI to front the show with ticket and album giveaways and the usual hundreds of plugs.

Day after day went by with no mention of the Beach Boys on WCPO. An article in the newspaper headlined, "Best kept secret, Beach Boys Coming To Town." a few days prior to the event finally jolted management, the sales department, and the concert promoter into rage-filled action. The lackadaisical PD quickly recruited Bob Keith to record several screaming announcements about the concert and we began a phone-in contest promising free tickets, complete Beach Boy album collections, cash money and the kitchen sink but it was too late to have much effect and the group played to a sparse crowd.

My friend Shad O' Shea was our next PD and he did his best under the circumstances. In addition to our weak signal, management had cut our promotion and contest budget to the bone. It seems they had blown about ten years worth in our debut blitz that fizzled following the tragic assassination of JFK.

I just kept going to work and having a grand old time playing the hits and striving to entertain from midnight to six, then 7 P M to midnight for a while then back to the all night show. It didn't matter as long as I was on the air. I figured my job was secure as long as I could avoid being promoted to Program Director.

The title of Program Director should really be Fall Guy. He takes the rap for all bad ratings while upper management grabs the credit for good ones. Some stations now have a ridiculous chain of command with fall guys under fall guys under fall guys. For instance, General Manager and Vice President, and under him, Station Manager, then Operations Manager, next, Program Director, finally Assistant Program Director unless he holds out for an assistant.

Who Are You, Who, Who?

Morton Downey was an old-time Irish tenor and a big radio star in his day. When his son was making national news, not always in a way that the father approved of, he told an inquiring reporter, "There is no Morton Downey Jr." This started the tale that an imposter was trying to cash in on Morton Downey's fame. This was only partially true. The young man was Downey's son, but his real name was Sean, not Morton.

Sean, or Mort as we called him, joined the staff of WCPO in 1964. Rex Jones brought him in to fill the afternoon drive slot. He liked to call himself Doc Downey since he used the initials M. D. Mort was the most talented, energetic, charismatic and creative DJ I ever knew and I have worked with several of America's best. He was a musician who could sing, play several instruments and compose music. He wrote Pipeline, recorded by The Chantays, Wipeout by the Safaris and had numerous hit records that he performed.

Lorne Greene of Bonanza fame had a recitation hit titled Ringo and I wrote a spoof of it, replacing the gun-slinging Ringo in the original version with Ringo Starr. During Beatlemania about all one had to do was mention a Beatle's name to cash in. Mort liked the lyrics and we booked a session at a recording studio in Dayton. Shad O' Shea, another experienced record producer, joined us on the trip.

We arrived early enough to grab dinner at a family restaurant and as we were being seated in the crowded place, Mort began his act, tripping and doing a loud prat fall in between tables, knocking utensils and condiments flying. Now that he had captured everyone's attention he kept the performance going, pretending to be mentally handicapped and barely able to speak. Mort had a denture plate which he removed to make himself look more goofy and continued to mug and rant loudly throughout the meal.

He ordered fried onions, broke one in half, stripped off the coating, stuck one end up a nostril and walked around asking startled strangers, "Excuse me, do you have a handkerchief?" Shad and I were not above clowning ourselves and though we couldn't avoid laughing, we were totally embarrassed and grossed out.

Things didn't go great at the recording studio as the guy we worked with had unbelievably never heard the Lorne Greene record, a smash hit that every station was playing in hot rotation. When I tried to perform my version in a similar style and tempo of the original, he would stop taping and coach me to do it in a sing-song manner. We left with what I considered a piece of, shall we say trash? Mort played it a lot on his show and it was popular in Cincinnati for a few weeks in spite of itself. However, my dreams of a potential nationwide hit novelty record went the way of most releases which is nowhere. All I retained was an everlasting memory of Morton Downey Jr. with a stripped onion ring dangling from his nose. Yes, I'll have fries with mine for life.

Mort was an excellent, high energy DJ who knew how to get ratings. He recruited his own army of teenage fans and ran a weekly hop featuring live bands. A battle of the bands was conducted each week. The winners would be named house band and paid a few bucks until defeated. The other bands left disappointed. Mort judged the winners and losers by the kid's cheers and applause. He of course rigged the results and thereby had the benefit of several unpaid bands each week. I filled in for him a couple of times when he was out of town and once while he was going around and around night and day at Coney Islands Amusement Park, setting the world's record for marathon Ferris wheel rides. I conducted the dances accompanied by his gorgeous and gracious wife. Mort said that I was the only guy on the staff he trusted with her. I'm not sure if that was a compliment. Naturally Mort instructed me to make sure his house band won.

Mort was an emotional man and could display a volatile temper when upset. He was hyper-active on the air, blasting the studio monitors at full volume and beating pens to pieces as he drummed along with the music. Shad and Mike once decided to play a little prank on him by tossing a huge firecracker under his chair. The cement block wall was barely three feet behind the studio chair and when the cherry bomb exploded the noise was enough to bust one's ear drums. Mort erupted from the chair in a blind rage. He grabbed the heavy, soundproof studio door and ripped it off its hinges. He then stalked down the hall searching for the culprit who had set off the explosion. Fortunately Shad and Mike had made their getaway. As rapidly as he had gone into a rage, Mort calmed down and accepted the trick as a good stunt. Shad and Mike both came back and apologized as an engineer was re-hanging the door. Mort told them there were no hard feelings, but if he had caught someone at the time he would have ripped out his testicles and crammed them down his throat. Seeing what happened to the door, I didn't doubt him.

Downey was easily bored and amid the British Invasion fad and despite his successful show he was stricken with a brainstorm to call himself Doctor Dee from London, England and assign Morton Downey Jr. to a Saturday weekend show only. Speaking or more like yelling in a raucous voice Doctor Dee usurped afternoon drive. Calls poured in complaining that the good doctor sounded nothing like a British citizen and they wanted Mort back. The Dee character yelled insults and hung up on them. After about a week, the Assistant GM Bob Gordon ordered Downey to bag the Dee character because they were paying Morton Downey Jr. to do the show not some obnoxious imposter. Doctor Dee announced he was making a quick trip back to Jolly Old England and that he would mail a card from there to anyone sending him a card before he departed. The mail poured in addressed to Doctor Dee and Downey attempted to use them as evidence that the character was too popular to cancel. It didn't work and Mort was about ready to take his act on the road again.

Mort was a generous guy to those he liked and he dropped by the station now and then when I was still writing full time and would invite me to join him for lunch at a certain, up-scale restaurant. The owners always greeted him like the big-time celebrity he claimed to be and he had them falling over themselves to please him.

Mort would ask to just sign the check as they let him run a tab. He would be sure to add a very nice tip before signing, then ask the beaming waitress if the manager would cash a small, personal check for him since he was a little short of cash. No problem. They were willing to do anything to keep Morton Downey's son as a regular customer.

A month or two later I heard the office gossip about Mort being hauled into court for failure to pay a rather large restaurant bill. The case was dismissed when he showed the judge canceled checks for amounts slightly higher than the tabs bearing the same dates.

Despite good ratings, the ever-restless Downey took off for his next job after only a few months. He headed to WFUN, Miami where Bob Keith had worked. Later he had a whirlwind career in politics, went into talk radio, then a talk show on TV and landed several movie and TV acting roles. He delved in professional sports franchises, helping to bring a basketball team to New Orleans, had a part in forming the WBO boxing organization and World League Baseball. His four packs a day smoking habit finally killed him in 2001.

SIX

You Just Keep Me Hanging On

We were rockin' and rollin' trying our best with Shad at the helm when out of the blue in the fall of '65 it was announced that the station had been sold. A little surprise is good for the system. Word came down that a company based in Seattle had purchased the AM and FM facilities and would broadcast from new studios downtown. The memo from management was the standard crock of sewage stating that no changes in personnel were anticipated and that anyone bailing out prematurely would not receive severance pay. Translation: Start preparing an audition tape and a resume immediately!

The new guys came in and canned everyone but me. No one had spoken to me in advance and I was pondering a move to Baltimore where Bob Keith had accepted a Program Director position and he asked me to join him. The GM there wanted me to move my family, which by now consisted of a wife and three small children for the same salary I was making in Cincinnati. He sounded like a pompous character over the phone and I turned down the offer. The station, WITH was another low-powered peanut cooker on the same frequency as WCPO and management would undoubtedly expect miracles as had the Scripps Howard brain trust prior to tossing in the towel. Upper management had been ashamed of Top 40 radio from the beginning and it took no genius to realize that they had only hoped to build up the ratings for a more profitable sale.

While we were being lied to about no big changes anticipated, the new owners had their staff housed in a downtown hotel ready to go on air as soon as the deal was final. Somebody had to keep the needle peaking.

Their National Program Director, Pat O 'Day loved my air work and at the first WUBE staff meeting he stated that I was one of the top all-night jocks in America, possibly the best. He must have caught my show on a good night. Maybe he was the one drinking tequila when he listened. Whatever, it saved me from moving to a faraway place for a job that wouldn't have lasted very long as Bob Keith was to soon leave Baltimore and go back home to Miami, Florida. A couple of the new jocks resented me because they wanted one of their friends to work the all-night show, or maybe they wanted someone they hated to be sentenced to the all-night show. The call letters were changed to WUBE, nearly impossible to pronounce smoothly.

O' Day, several years ahead of his time, chose them deliberately in order for the station to be known as 1, 2, 3 W B. It cleverly named our location on the dial and included the letters phonetically. In stodgy Cincy this did not go over well. Many callers and people on the streets mumbled that they were not going to listen to us because a radio station was supposed to have at least three letters.

Pat O' Day was an innovator who should have launched his idea in a more hip market. Today it is a rare station that does not identify itself by dial position and some variance of call letters only. If one station in a big market decides to call itself Scabies Radio and gets ratings, there will be at least 749 Scabies Radio stations within a month.

You Ain't Goin'Nowhere

At the demise of WCPO radio most of the DJs scattered to other on-air jobs, but a couple of guys hung up the old headphones permanently. Shad O' Shea went into the insurance business for a few years then opened a recording studio. He had grown weary of radio and producing records and writing books was his true passion. Mike Gavin also stayed in Cincinnati, moving across town as an account executive in the sales department of WLW where he enjoyed a lucrative career. Dick Provost had gone to WBZ, Boston, Myles Foland ended up at a station in central Florida and Jack McCoy snagged the all-night show at WCKY for a while. Rock Robins, a terrific evening DJ, had been long gone to a station in Detroit where fortunately he shed the avian moniker and operated under the name of Scott Regan.

I had either moved to a new job or not. There were new call letters, new studios and new co-workers but with the same old weak signal on the same old frequency as I worked the same old shift in the same city. I was quite happy to be involved in the exciting new venture and couldn't understand how a couple of excellent DJs like Shad and Mike could walk away from such a great way to make a living. Who needs decent pay and job security?

The new WUBE studios were located on the second floor of the Fifth Third Bank. You needed a calculator to find the place. There we were in downtown Cincinnati across from the main Post Office with an entrance in the alley between the two buildings. We had roomy studios and offices unlike the old digs and I did not miss those snug accommodations.

National Program Director Pat O' Day and WUBE PD Ken Dowe had brought in a talented group of on-air people to replace a talented group. Their reasoning was to feature a whole new station, DJs, news readers, office staff, sales department and call letters. Retaining me as the overnight personality obviously irritated Dowe and he snubbed me except for a couple of wee hour phone calls accusing me of some format violation. Before he could garner enough evidence, real or imagined to convince O' Day that I should be fired and after just two weeks in the Queen City he walked out in a snit after a disagreement with management. He was among the first of several to cause me to adopt the self-assuring motto; I was here before he arrived and I'll be here after he's gone.

Wake Me Up Before You Go Go

The new morning man was another extremely rare talent on the order of Morton Downey Jr. He used his full name of Rex Miller Spangberg on the air since Cincinnati was home to many thousands with German heritage. I had enjoyed listening to him when he was Rex Miller on KWK, St. Louis. Clever, funny, witty, creative, whip smart, you name it and he had it. Rex wrote satirical books and articles, recorded comedy records and grabbed big ratings wherever he was on the air. Even though I was pretty well worn out and hungry as he relieved me each weekday morning at 6 A M, I liked to hang around for an hour or two with him as he did his show.

Rex was really into the James Bond secret agent craze which was hot at that time. He would arrive in a dark suit and tie wearing a fedora hat. He always carried a small valise with his show material inside. He told me that he always wrote for a year ahead. Each evening, while enjoying a few cocktails he would hammer out jokes and routines for exactly one year from the next morning. That's unique.

Rex was also a gifted ad-libber who could improvise comedy at a second's notice. He possessed a sense of humor that was a little on the dark and twisted side of life. I was somewhat unnerved one morning when showed me that his briefcase contained a hand grenade and a semi-automatic handgun equipped with an illegal silencer. He seemed to really want a mugger to attack him in the alley or for some threatening lunatic to break in while he was on the air. He was a huge man who liked to practice karate chops and kicks on the studio walls so I'm sure no mugger or even a seriously deranged show critic would dare challenge even an unarmed Rex Miller Spangberg.

Rex garnered good ratings but could not resist testing the limits with sarcastic remarks. Frustrated with the station's lack of power, he announced a contest with prizes consisting of maps of our overage area printed on postage stamps. The General Manager of the month immediately fired him which pleased Rex to no end since he had in his possession a hand-written contract from Ken Dowe assuring him of a year's salary if he was fired. The GM snickered, thinking it worthless, but a judge ruled in favor of Rex. It seems a few words scrawled on a sheet of paper torn from a legal-size writing tablet are indeed legal.

The original 1 2 3 WB staff did not last long. Within just a few months, in addition to Rex and Ken Dowe, Mac Hudson, Jim Horne and Frank Benny had all vamoosed. I just kept on playing the hits doing the bits and keeping the needle peaking on the all-night show. Job hopping was not my thing once I got into radio. Some DJs spend their entire careers going from one station to the next perpetually seeking those greener pastures which are never found. They should be smarter than cattle.

Disc Jockeys have on-air personae which may reflect their true personalities or they may be totally false. Some of the most overbearing, sarcastic, mean-spirited broadcasters are actually as nice as can be off the air. Conversely, some of the sneakiest, low-life scum in the business pretend to be as sweet and benevolent as Mother Teresa's Holy apple pie once they crack a microphone. Either way, no one can do a show every day without automatically assuming an on-air persona that differs to some extent from his or her normal behavior. It may not change one quite as much as a TV camera does, but the difference is there. It's acting.

Some Jocks never excel because they are afraid to offend. Few of them ever advance beyond a shift where the only requirement is to push start buttons and two or three times an hour read a station positioning statement such as "Shauntavius Radio, at 87 point 9 plays more of the most, best, favorite, newest, non-stop music." I was never reluctant to offend since a certain amount of radio listeners are already offended by your name, the call letters, the jingles, the music, the static, the news, and most of all the commercials. The facts are indisputable that the most offensive Jocks in America are the most successful and best paid. I just wasn't gross or belligerent enough to get rich as a DJ. I tried.

Some DJs are real music freaks. They love to turn the studio monitors and their headphones to the very highest, deafening volumes so they can "feel" or "really get into" the music. If you ask them for any further details they will inevitably answer with, "Huh?"

If they are crazy about the music they are usually lousy DJs because they will over-play their favorites, refuse to play others that are in the rotation, smuggle in music not on the playlist and constantly whine about what the station is and isn't playing. They can't comprehend that the station is not their personal Ipod. Unless you are the General Manager in a very small market and can order the DJs to play your favorites, even if they be Lawrence Welk and Hawaiian music, it is far better to just play the legitimate hits.

Despite research which can cost a station hundreds of thousands of dollars a year, expensive consultants, nagging Program Directors and common sense, the less music a morning DJ or team plays the higher the ratings. The quickest way to destroy a successful morning show is to cut back on the jokes and celebrity gossip to add more music but unless a Jock has the right to play or not play music written into a contract, he will be ordered to play more and more music and to talk less until the ratings are destroyed. Researchers almost always provide management with data that says listeners want less talk and more music. A careful follow up into those surveys would reveal that the audience defines "talk" as commercials and news, and not necessarily DJ chatter. The same listeners who complain about too much talk complain more because the DJs don't announce the artists and song titles.

SEVEN

Let the Good Times Roll

The owners of WUBE were Lester Smith and Danny Kaye, the actor. Home base was in Seattle where the company owned the successful rocker KJR. Many thought our W B stood for Warner Brothers but it didn't. Why Pat O' Day picked WUBE for call letters remains a mystery other than it rhymes with 1, 2, 3 and our frequency was 1230. Danny Kaye only visited one time and his stay was brief. After a quick tour of the studios he shrugged and mumbled, "Big (expletive deleted) deal." There's nothing like receiving a rousing endorsement and pep talk from the owner.

The passing parade of DJs and General Managers continued for the next few years. I was moved to the mid day shifts of nine to noon, then noon to three, and finally mornings from six to nine. One manager declared the staff to be The All Americans and we were required to dress alike with blue Polo shirts bearing red, white and blue logos, along with white pants and black shoes. The new boss was declaring war on the growing hippie image in America by demanding we be clean-cut, short-haired, close- shaved ideal patriots. Before or after our air shifts we were to drive around town in a red, white and blue station van handing out trinkets and phoning in reports. He also closely monitored all the music, turning thumbs down on anything that was the slightest bit suggestive or sounded psychedelic to his ultra-conservative ears. This pruned the standard Top 40 down to perhaps a Top 27. He left after a few months and we reverted to dressing like slobs and playing the hits.

Our lineup in those days featured Wayne Shane, Big Al Law Brady, Bwana Johnny, Dusty Dunn, and me. We were called in for a staff meeting and it was announced that a new Program Director from the Drake/Chenault organization would be installing a new system. Bill Drake the, programming expert had been achieving great success with the RKO station chain in such markets as Los Angeles, New York City, Memphis and San Francisco. Finally, it looked as if we were going to stop fumbling around and put some heat on big, bad WSAI.

The Drake format was simple but effective and worked like magic when closely followed. Countless stations tried to copy it but by omitting some of the nuances it never worked as well as the original. The format limited commercials, added music sweeps, moved the news to twenty minutes past and twenty minutes prior to each hour and cut DJ chatter to the bare minimum. They said it over the record intro, over the music fade or they'd better not say it at all. In just a few weeks and for the first time ever we were nipping at the heels of WSAI. The station went back to calling itself WUBE and management opened up the vault to provide a huge contest budget. We were called the Boss Jocks, sometimes with a straight face. The term Boss was hokey even in the 60s but somehow it worked, so we were Boss Radio.

Programmers who tried to imitate the Drake format ran into opposition from management and sales who rarely allowed them to limit commercials. Most refused to move newscasts from their traditional on the hour and half-hour positions. Drake's 20/20 news allowed music sweeps across the tops and bottoms of the hour while the competition was airing news, a proven tune out and just something that had to be tolerated to pacify the FCC.

Contradictory to our previous GM, the Drake people preferred us to stay hidden. I believe it was because one of our best personalities, a clever, hip, fast-talking young guy who called himself Bwana Johnny was just over five feet tall and weighed three hundred pounds. Drake's theory was that each listener drew a mental image of a DJ and it was best not to puncture those illusions. The brains in the company ordered Bwana to drop his on-air name claiming that it could be offensive to African-Americas. He called himself Johnny Johnson for a week or two until overwhelming negative reaction from the audience forced them to rescind their order. It seems that folks of all races liked the name Bwana Johnny and didn't dig Johnny Johnson.

Radio Is Forever?
Wowee, Pretty Scary

Disc Jockeys work conscientiously for hours then the show ends and they are left with a feeling of emptiness. All the clever quips, great music mixes and tightly controlled console operations are gone without a trace. Well, not really. Theoretically radio waves continue to travel through space at the speed of light until the end of time, including all of that negative gobbledygook I used to pull on the all-night show. The thought gives me some satisfaction since most of my graveyard shift schedules were a fly by night Program Director's method of punishment. If I told any jokes deemed too negative or violated a precious format I was assigned the midnight to 6 A.M. show where I immediately broke every rule in the book. A new PD would soon be hired and inevitably he would ask, "Hey, what's our best Jock doing on the all night show," and promote me to the morning shift.

Somewhere out in space, perhaps a trillion miles past Jupiter there is the late night ad lib I uttered. It was a dark and stormy night. Suddenly my voice rang out, "It's mighty quiet around here. Come on over and we'll have a party."

Within the next hour the light bulb that signaled someone pressing the doorbell downstairs began flashing. Eventually, I put on one of our longer all-time great musical masterpieces and took the elevator down to check things out. Gathered around the double glass doors were about a dozen members of a motorcycle gang with their "old ladies" demanding to be let in to join the party.

Occasionally someone takes a stupid DJ remark seriously. Changing my voice into my best technical Nerd imitation, I yelled that the show was on tape, I was just the engineer, not responsible for content and no Disc Jockey was on duty. I hustled back upstairs as they cursed and mumbled threats. Thankfully they left without destroying the building. I learned to refrain from inviting guests to the studios and reminded myself that no matter how weak the signal or how bad programming may be, someone just might be listening.

How can we smugly ignore the possibility, a remote one I will concede that some alien equivalent of a biker gang billions of light years from earth just might be scanning the dial on the AM band, hear my old invitation and decide to join the party? What are the chances they would leave peacefully after traveling from the far ends of the universe only to discover that they have been duped? I'm confident they would annihilate humanity starting with Disc Jockeys. That is if such creatures have not already been totally wiped out by greedy group station owners. They are definitely an endangered species.

Such irresponsible comments as mine led to the restrictions of present day radio which dictate, no ad libs, just read the positioning statements (silly slogans) where scheduled and try to stay awake. If they cut voice tracks on a computer and are not even in the station, some poor engineer may actually take the rap for my thoughtless comment. That would be fair retribution since such techno geeks invented those everlasting, universe-polluting radio waves.

The Hits Just Kept On Coming.
Uh, Oh, Check That

After a futile five years of humiliation at the hands of WSAI the curse had apparently been lifted and little old, under-powered WUBE was about to take over the number one position in the market for Top 40 radio. The keen teens had stopped referring to us as copycats and we were beating WSAI in certain day parts with that target audience. Bill Drake then made a serious strategic blunder. He decided that we had already won the battle for the teens and it was time to program for an older audience.

We dropped several of the more raucous hits, added more ballads by older artists and instituted a three in a row segue format with no talk between records. The bottom fell out of the ratings as the teen audience kissed us off and no adults showed up to replace them. Shortly thereafter the Drake/Chenault programming agreement expired and WUBE went back to the Program Director, General Manager merry go round and it's accompanying dismal ratings.

Bill Drake's real name was Phillip Yarbrough and he changed it to rhyme with wake when he was a DJ and Program Director at WAKE, Atlanta. After making the station number one, he was transferred to KYA in San Francisco where he again took the station to the top. While at KYNO, Fresno, he met and partnered up with Gene Chenault. They perfected the Top 40 format by cleaning up the on-air clutter and by taking the programming reins out of the hands of the sales departments.

Drake had also shocked and amazed less astute programmers by putting his Top 40 format on WOR-FM in New York City with great success. Imagine that, something other than dismal elevator music on an FM station. Shocked out of their stupor, programmers all over the country soon had converted their formerly near-worthless FM properties into music stations, albeit mostly with album music and whispering, pseudo-hippie DJs rather than high energy Top 40 personalities.

The cursed WUBE AM mistake was the only Bill Drake goof I ever heard of. I was starting to wonder if it was my fault since I was the only on-air constant from the Fun radio debut through the sale, change of call-letters and countless formats. I have harbored a suspicion that Drake was using WUBE as an experiment and since it was not an RKO station, his major client, no big loss if the format change failed.

Drake's Program Director, Nick Anthony left to continue working with the company and Al Law Brady was hired to move to WOR-FM. Disc Jockeys and Program Directors came and went and I just kept on plugging away, still enjoying being on the air.

One character whose name shall go unmentioned because he used a generic one claimed by many others and I don't want to start rumors about the wrong guys, was the most obnoxious of all the people I ever worked with. He was married but showed up at station promotions with a 14 year old girlfriend. He bought a brown Nehru suit which was a fad at the time, and wore it every single day. I followed him on the air and he always signed off by telling his few listeners that there would be no good music until he returned the next day so they should turn off their radios. He was one of the Jocks ensnared by a perverted couple in an attempted extortion. Stay tuned.

Program Directors tend to mistakenly gauge a DJ's performance and the size of the audience by telephone activity. Therefore, stations have what is sarcastically called a request line, though a request is never answered unless by pure luck that particular number happens to be coming up in the rotation. Actually playing what the public requests would quickly lead to the most horrific mishmash of novelty songs and unintelligible gibberish since Inna Gadda Da Vidi.

Someone should tell programming wizards that people who call radio stations are generally a small group of misfits with nothing else to do with no one else to talk to. When the station is giving away something to callers, greedy cheats phone constantly hoping to win a prize. These are the good callers, the cream of the crop. The others are a mix of belligerent miscreants who only call to tell the Jocks how horrible their station is and to threaten violence if they don't play some obscure song, and of course desperate females who like to talk dirty. The latter are especially abundant during a full moon. I soon learned that the lunar cycle was the cue for lunatics to stay awake all night and call radio stations.

Answering crackpot calls by the thousands over the years was more than enough to convince me that Alexander Graham Bell was a Satanist. Every control room also has a dreaded hotline with a supposedly top-secret number that only staff members have privy to. These bright red torture devices are used for one purpose only; to make the lives of DJs miserable. Some programmers and their bosses think they are not being diligent unless they call the Jock on duty and whine about something they heard, real or imagined. The highly secret numbers have a way of becoming widespread knowledge as guys give them to their girlfriends or groupies. It was rather annoying to answer a hotline call, brace oneself for a chewing out as a PD tried to impress his wife, date or drinking buddies only to hear, "Um, um, would you play that new song by The Monkees?"

Several reports claim that children exposed to music education at a very early age perform better in school. Something about rhythms and patterns in music teach them to organize their thoughts while enhancing their memories. I remain skeptical. How can a kid solve a math problem for example, while some wacky song is running through his head? It is an irritating syndrome known as an ear worm. The harder one tries to get a crazy tune off his mind, the more persistently the beat goes on.

Education experts maintain that classical music is especially good for improving the brain. To kids nowadays classical music is something by the Rolling Stones. I spent many years answering so-called request lines and it was obvious that smart kids were not calling. Most of the young music freaks would wait until I was playing some obnoxious, teenie-bopper stiff then call and request it while it was still spinning. With some of today's raunchy, obscene lyrics, I believe that children should not be exposed to music prior to voting age.

Late night TV commercials may be behind this scheme for kiddy brain boosting, as they attempt to sell musty copies of Mozart, Beethoven, Jim Nabors and George Jones CDs that have been gathering mold in warehouse basements. Small children are already bombarded with tunes by Barney and Friends, Hannah Montana, Puff Daddy and the theme from Empire Carpets, yet in my observation of neighborhood tots I have noticed no evidence of genius.

If children are exposed to classical music and by some miracle happen to like it, past experience warns me that instead of whining for electrified guitars, huge amplifiers and a touring bus, they will throw tantrums and demand expensive violins, cellos, pianos and tubas before they enter pre-school.

My final piece of evidence proving that classical music does not make one smarter is my old report card from the year I was required to take Music Appreciation. I not only flunked the course, I became so confused trying to remember all those foreign names I almost flunked history too.

Posing as a lonely housewife one woman called the DJs almost daily and would quickly lead them into a conversation about meeting for a wild encounter, asking for their most detailed fantasies of what they would do during the tryst. I hated phones by then and despised answering the fake request line but the bosses always insisted that we answer every call and to be sugary-sweet and accommodating to the precious listeners no matter how infuriating or obnoxious they might be. Sorry, but I am only nice to those who are nice to me. I still hate phones, will always hate phones, don't own a cell phone and wouldn't have a so-called land phone if I could convince my wife that we don't need it. If I ever said, "It's me or the phone," well, some things are better left unsaid.

Meanwhile, the horny lady kept calling every DJ on the staff but me after I tried popping a few jokes and making fun of her. I'm no angel, but I just didn't care to talk to that woman while trying to do a show. A fellow jock somehow discovered that while she was making her provocative calls, dear hubby was listening for kicks on an extension. This was their way of spicing up the old marital routine. Then one of them had another idea.

Hubby had not only been listening in, he had also been taping the calls. A lawyer representing the couple contacted management with an offer to turn over the tapes for $350,000 in lieu of contacting the authorities, claiming that the Jocks had kept her phone number after she entered a contest and that they had been placing obscene calls to her.

A meeting was held, presided over by the stern and humorless co-owner, Lester Smith, and every DJ except me had to give a sworn deposition that they had placed no calls and had only answered the phone. I was thankful for my aversion to phones. The station's lawyer threatened to have the creepy couple charged with extortion and they decided to let bygones be bygones.

Goin' Up Country

About a year after the Drake/Chenault experiment the owners threw in the Top 40 towel and we learned that the station was switching to Country music. The new Program Director dropped into the studio while I was on the air, observed me answering the "request" line while music played and mused, "Those phones are a big distraction." I thought, "You don't know the half of it."

It's just one little surprise after another in the radio biz. Following five and a half years of keeping the needle peaking with the latest pop hits at 1230 on the dial, the owners had decided to bring in a Country programmer. None of the Jocks were thrilled to say the least, but it was actually a wise move since there was no established Country music station in the city, and they had finally admitted that our feeble signal could not compete with WSAI.

Advertising agencies have strong tendencies to purchase air time only on the leading station in each genre. WSAI was going to continue to get the Top 40 buys, but now WUBE could expect to benefit from those desiring to reach Country music fans.

Deja Vu and all that stuff as every DJ except me was handed a severance check. Maybe I looked and sounded countrified enough for the new Program Director or maybe I had been loyal to the owners through so many changes they didn't have the heart to fire me, in any case I was soon playing Merle Haggard and Loretta Lynn instead of The Beatles and Sam The Sham.

As I worked the late evening shift while spinning downbeat drinking and cheating songs in an empty building, it almost caused me to long for my old nemesis, the request line. I take that back. It wasn't that bad, but I was elated and excited when George Burns, National Program Director for the company that owned WSAI called me at home and requested a meeting to discuss a job.

It wasn't just a job, it was the Program Director position at WQXI, Atlanta a national leader in Top 40 radio, located in a town I loved and where Dixie's parents lived. Burns sent me flying to Atlanta to meet with the General Manager, Jerry Blum. He interviewed me, gave his approval and I was hired.

My Country Jock career had lasted two weeks and then I was back in the rock and roll game. Burns had admired my sense of humor and creativity at WUBE which I never stopped practicing through the ups and downs of WCPO and WUBE. I kept myself entertained and sometimes lots of other people. WUBE did pretty well as a Country station and when they finally decided to put the format on their much more powerful FM facility they became an influential Country station.

Owners and management of FM facilities may have been slow to realize their potential, but FM receivers were scarce in homes and practically non-existent in automobiles prior to the 1970's. There also existed widespread snobbery which dictated that FM's superior quality was too good for rock or Country music. This lasted right up until Bill Drake put Boss radio on WOR FM and the FM brass across the country realized they were sitting on potential goldmines. I wouldn't have been shocked if FM stations switching formats to Top 40 had organized protests, burning piles of Montovani, Lawrence Welk, Hawaiian and Big Band records. I would have gladly supplied the kerosene.

EIGHT

She's Not There

Arriving for duty April 15, 1969 I was pleasantly surprised to see that WQXI was everything I had been told, with a beautiful, colorful reception area prominently displaying a huge station logo, adjoining studios where visitors could observe the DJs and news reporters in action and nothing but well-dressed, attractive people arriving at work with smiles on their faces. Amazing what a top-rated, financially solid operation can due for morale. One immediately sensed that WQXI was a Top 40 station and proud of the title. It was the kind of station I had been expecting to see when I went to Cincinnati but failed to find.

The second person I met after checking in with the receptionist was a lovely young girl named Virginia Byrd. She introduced herself as my secretary. Imagine me in charge of programming with my own personal secretary and an office. Well, sort of. The office was a WCPO radio sized room with one desk and a chair and one additional chair for the secretary.

"Where do you do your typing," I inquired.

"Oh, I can't type," she replied with a giggle. I was starting to come down just a bit from my initial happy rush.

I was quickly assured that the small office was temporary and that the big boss and President of programming for the Pacific and Southern chain of stations, Kent Burkhart and National Program Director George Burns would soon be moving into even more luxurious offices a short distance up Peachtree Street. General Manager Jerry Blum would then move into Burkhart's old office and I would get Jerry's vacated space.

My 19 year old, non-typing, non-shorthand-taking thus non-dictation capable secretary was cute with a cheerful personality but I couldn't quite figure out why the interim PD, Barry Chase, had hired her. Some gossipy staff members soon informed me that Barry wanted to retain the Program Director's job on a permanent basis, at least as permanent as radio programming jobs can be, and he hired Virginia because her step-father was the President of the corporation. Barry had the mistaken notion that she could provide job security. Barry was a fine disc jockey but management was unhappy with his performance as a programmer. I landed the job and inherited his secretary.

The young lady's presence made management quite uncomfortable;

believing that she might be spilling too many inside details to the company President and quite fearful of the consequences should one of the Disc Jockeys become involved in a scandal with her. I could understand their concern along those lines, having worked with some of the most rabid, skirt-chasing hedonists outside of a Roman fertility festival. Burns let me know that it was my duty to baby-sit her.

Did I mention that the job of Program Director should bear the sub-title, Fall Guy? One of my first assignment as a major market PD was the first of many unpleasant duties, firing someone. Who was going to put his neck on the line by firing the big boss's daughter? I liked the girl and enjoyed her company even if she was not a real secretary and dreaded giving her the bad news. She loved the station, the music and the job.

The company also owned WQXI-TV Channel 11 at the time and with a little prompting from Kent Burkhart and Jerry Blum the TV station agreed to give her a job. I was able to convince her that she was not being fired from radio but promoted to television. It worked out wonderfully as she quickly blossomed as a TV personality. After a few shots on Channel 11, she was hired as a weather reporter at WAGA TV then became the host of the entertainment show P M Magazine under her married name, Virginia Gunn. Instead of hating me, we remained friends and she later aired a couple of segments on me in my Red Neckerson character.

When Virginia left, the receptionist was selected by management to be my secretary. It didn't work out as she liked to party a little too hard at night and would miss work frequently. I was urged to fire her by higher ups then was chewed out for taking their advice. I went for several weeks with no secretary as applicants were either pitifully inept or expecting at least twice what the job paid. My secretary's main and near sole responsibility was to answer the phone. Phones I hate, typing I liked to do myself. I have to see where I am on paper and do not like to dictate anything longer than a short message or lunch order.

I had moved into the fancy office and the secretary had her own desk, phone and typewriter in an adjoining area. I interviewed an attractive lady who seemed intelligent enough and who was willing to accept the salary offered. I hired her and soon learned to my dismay that she was a slow learner. Perhaps she was a non-learner. The phones had several lines that could be accessed by punching the correct buttons. When a call came in, a light would flash signaling which button to push. She could not understand such a complicated process. She would pick up the phone and start talking to either a dial tone or interrupt a call to the General Manager or Sales Manager's office. No matter how many times I explained it to her, she never solved the problem.

Since she was doing nothing but causing havoc, I asked her to bring me something from the concession stand located on the first floor. She was gone for hours and I thought she had decided to quit and had walked out never to return. No such luck. Finally, a short while before the end of the work day she returned to tell me that she had met this nice man in the elevator and they had spent the afternoon together. She told me that her father was a strict preacher and then she had married a straight-laced, controlling man. Now that she was divorced and free, she was making up for lost time. She lasted from Monday through Friday only because I didn't want to admit to being a totally lousy judge of intellect and character. My third secretary Susan Jones, was hired only after approval by Jerry Blum and several women staffers. Susan was an efficient, happily married wife and mother whom I wish had come along a few weeks earlier.

What'd I Say Parts 1 & 2
The Real Skinny on Harper

Along with Barry Chase, the DJ staff included Bob Bolton, Randy Robins Brother Lee Love and morning man "Skinny" Bobby Harper. Skinny he was, of average height and the wearer of coke bottle thick eye-glasses. Bobby had worked at WSAI while I was in Cincinnati so I was quite familiar with his on-air style. He was funny, inventive and often outrageous, testing the patience of management. He was even wilder in his free time, drinking beer and driving like a lunatic.

The audience, ad agencies and the General Manager loved him, but Kent Burkhart did not care for his antics. Shortly after I had notified Virginia Byrd of her "promotion," I was directed to fire Harper at his next slightly off-color or distasteful joke. Since I had been contributing many of his one-liners and routines this was not welcome news. I liked Bobby and thought he was an excellent DJ. He worked hard at preparing material and mapping out his show every night. Often he would phone me at home, tell me he needed some lines about a current event and say, "I'll call you back in a half hour."

Since I was technically his boss I could have refused, but I enjoyed writing humor and he knew if someone gives me a topic I can give them a joke. Occasionally I went on the air with him performing character voices. Despite his popularity and excellent ratings I was goaded into firing him, or else.

Jerry Blum was furious, the advertisers were irate and the listeners were, let's say teed off. Following a few days of angry phone calls and near mutiny from the office workers, management and programming met with Bobby. He was allowed to plead his case and he promised to be a good boy. He was reinstated and I was ordered to keep a close ear on him in case he might tell another of his alleged dirty jokes that in reality would not offend a Pentecostal congregation.

For the next couple of weeks it seemed like my phone rang every other time Skinny Bobby opened his mouth with George Burns shouting, "Did you hear that? Did you hear what he said?" The game was rigged and I was soon ordered to fire Bobby for the final time.

For a while Bobby teamed with another ex-Quixie DJ and PD, Bob Todd in a pioneering TV venture. They had a weekend show on Atlanta's Channel 36 called TheNowExplosion, playing locally produced music videos of current hits along with humorous bits and DJ chatter. It was a great idea but ten years ahead of its time when more quality videos became available and MTV came along with a similar format. Bob Todd had been the last so-called permanent Program Director at Quixie prior to my being hired. Permanent meant until someone changed his mind.

Harper accepted a job in Louisville, Kentucky before returning to Atlanta and doing rather well at several other radio stations until he decided to retire from the radio business. He mellowed over the years both on and off the air. In his younger days he would agree to just about any crazy promotion or stunt, including one where he came near drowning in a giant bowl of Jello.

I hate firing anyone but unlike some cowardly wimps I have known, I can do it, face to face and as kindly and gently as possible. While in Cincinnati I observed weak-hearted administrators fire vacationing Jocks by slipping an envelope under their doors. This did nothing to add enjoyment or relaxation to a little time off.

Hiring and firing are big responsibilities and part of a leader's job. Anyone in charge of a department should either be capable of performing those duties in a professional manner or find another line of work. I always told the people I had to dismiss that it was opening new doors and creating opportunities for them and in almost all cases it proved to be true. Decide what you really want to do and what you are good at and pursue that goal. We are all born with latent abilities and the key to satisfaction is to use them.

Make Me Laugh

One thing I was in charge of as Program Director was coming up with something funny each day to be recorded and aired once an hour. These bits for some mysterious reason were called exotics. Maybe they couldn't think of any other title. Exotics could be take-offs on well-known TV commercials, movie or television show spoofs, fake interviews or any weird vignette dreamed up. Kent Burkhart and George Burns loved a good exotic and I could usually come up with one. Some days I called on certain DJs for suggestions. Mike Dineen and I spent some frustrating afternoons in my office racking our brains as we tried to come up with another thirty second comedy bit to entertain Burkhart and Burns. The radio audience we already had.

Bobby Harper had been replaced on the morning show by Simon Trane who had previously worked late evenings. I had hired Mike Dineen to do mornings out of Augusta, Georgia but he was soon moved to mid days mostly due to pressure from the gang of bosses who second-guessed my every decision. He is a great voice-over talent and was a big help with daily comedy material. He is also a fine Disc Jockey who went on to important jobs in top markets including New York City, St. Louis, Pittsburgh, Philadelphia and Houston. Evidently I wasn't the only one who thought he had talent.

I couldn't have been more naive about corporate politics or how a major market Program Director should operate. I realized that my comedy writing abilities had led to my being hired at WQXI just as they had taken me to WCPO. I had an innate gift for writing humorous stories that was discovered in English classes in both high school and college.

The first short story I turned in to my college English professor was about an amateur baseball player who wasn't very good but always had an alibi for his blunders. I was chagrined when my carefully crafted essay was returned bearing an F. After class I inquired of my middle-aged female instructor why the failing mark? She said it was because the story was not original. I insisted that it was. She then quizzed me like I was a special ed third grader, asking me to define words I had used in the story. I was able to do that quite easily, so reluctantly while shaking her head, she crossed out the F and scrawled a C on my paper. Since it was a composition class we had several more writing assignments and she soon realized I was not a plagiarist and began to adorn my efforts with As. Why she thought I was incapable of writing a couple of pages using big boy words I never understood. Maybe behind her thick glasses I just looked stupid.

Though I knew I could write short stories with a humorous bent, I never realized that I could write jokes until I tried. It's amazing how that works. While on my first job I had purchased a few books full of tired, corny jokes and had perused every so-called joke book in the local libraries with little luck. There were comedy services for DJs available but few of them were worth looking at and I couldn't afford them anyway. I had a sharp wit inherited from both of my wise-cracking parents and was able to ad lib some pretty funny lines at times but it is much better to have something prepared for those times when distractions and plain old down days stifle one's quick thinking.

Finding I could write one-liners and quick quips was a pleasant discovery. I had realized early on that announcers who just introduced records were headed down a dead end path. All the really successful and well-paid personalities came to work prepared. Egomaniacs who believed their dulcet tones and knowledge of the latest teen tunes would vault them to the top and keep them there were due a rude awakening. I was a good DJ with the ratings to prove it but I have always been better at writing.

It was quite easy to break into the radio business. It would also have been easy to be stuck in a minimum wage job for an entire career but I worked on my writing skills. I confess that some of my best work was completed while I was using a performance enhancing drug. Caffeine.

Over the years countless people have asked me "How do you do it? How do you come up with all that stuff? Can you tell me how to do it? Some have a hard time accepting the fact that a large part of it is being born with a perceptive sense of humor and the ability to see everything from a humorous angle. After that it requires work, practice and perseverance. Red Neckerson for instance was an overnight success only after I had put in twenty years of writing comedy for radio.

I have been asked to explain my creative side. Creativity consists of one-third imagination and two-thirds confidence with the courage to put one's unique ideas into action. Creativity is the opposite of playing follow the leader. I was lucky to work for people who appreciated my efforts and allowed me the freedom to express myself. It would have been even nicer if they had paid me more.

NINE

Cry Me a River
Capsizing a Raft of Misinformation

Reams have been written about the notorious Ramblin' Raft Race on the Chattahoochee River, most of the reports haphazardly or deliberately misleading as to how the event was born, how it grew into the largest outdoor sporting event in the world and how it expired. Accounts in the local newspapers and magazines and most Atlanta TV stations refused to include WQXI radio in their coverage of the events. The reason is simply because all media competes for the same advertising revenue and they sacrifice journalistic integrity in favor of money.

The hard facts are that without the involvement and promotion of WQXI radio and quite possibly without my approval of our participation in the first event there would never have been a newsworthy Chattahoochee Ramblin' Raft Race. I was involved at both the beginning and end of the phenomenon and I'm happy to set the record straight.

Most sloppy reports state that the event took place annually on Memorial Day weekend. It was actually on the third Saturday in May.

Our News Director Bob Neal, the most entertaining and creative radio news anchor I have ever heard, was a big asset to the morning show before he was stolen from us by our TV affiliate and eventually going on to national fame as a sportscaster for various television networks.

Bob received a call to the news room one morning in May, 1969 from a Georgia Tech student named Larry Patrick. As President of the Delta Sigma Phi fraternity he was issuing a challenge to the Quixie Jocks and all the other Tech fraternities to a paddle race down the Chattahoochee River. Larry had a fine feel for promotion and publicity and realized that without the enormously popular WQXI plugging the event it would receive no more than on-campus attention.

Neal, ever proficient at working in items of interest to our youthful audience, reported it in a newscast and added, "And Mike Dineen says he can beat any college boy paddling a raft down the Hooch."

Mike had recently taken over the morning show following the second departure of Skinny Bobby Harper and he went along with the bit. The gauntlet had been thrown down and accepted. During the day, Barry Chase, Bob Bolton and other DJs chimed in with jokes, taunts and preposterous statements about the now brewing contest. The guys came to me for approval to rent a four man raft. I gave the nod, but in the interest of truth, a so-called four man raft is not really big enough to accommodate four men unless perhaps they happen to be Danny Devito, Joe Pesci, Mini Me.and Vladimir Putin.

I received no objections from the three Bs, Blum, Burkhart and Burns, and soon young people in the metro area were excitedly organizing teams and preparing for a fun day on the river. In response to phone call requests, Larry Patrick and the DJs had invited anyone who wanted to compete to grab a raft and meet at the Morgan Falls Dam Saturday morning. The official count for registered floating devices the first year was 54.

Who knew? It appeared to be no more than another medium-sized Quixie DJ romp. No one had a clue of the exploding magnitude to come.

Atlanta was a youthful, partying city, bright, optimistic and ever-looking for uninhibited fun. With only a few days promotion on our highly-rated station, several teams showed up toting picnic baskets and coolers of beer, wine and other mood enhancers. Representing WQXI were Mike Dineen, Bob Bolton, Barry Chase and engineer Tom Giglio, a young, fun-loving guy who was not a typical acerbic technician with no time for frivolity. Their standard yellow blow-up raft proudly displayed the call letters constructed of duct tape.

Larry Patrick, somewhat overwhelmed at the turnout, realized that it would be impossible to conduct an actual race from start to finish because there were far too many rafts to allow a fair start in the narrow river. No problem, as nearly everyone excepting a few overly competitive types were only planning a leisurely social float down the Hooch, enjoying a laid-back day in the Georgia sunshine.

My participation in the initial raft race was minimal. I helped write some liners and promos and volunteered to drive the station van to the pickup point to haul the guys and their deflated raft back to their cars. The raft was not the only thing deflated when I found our tired, sun-burnt, soaking-wet crew. The six-mile float took several hours in the slow-moving current. All four men were exhausted from maneuvering through rapids, rocks, over-hanging tree branches and floating debris. A few beers each of them had consumed did not contribute to alertness and at least two guys fell asleep in the van on the way to the station.

When they had recovered the next day they were full of humorous tales to relate both on and off the air. The first of what was to become the annual Chattahoochee Ramblin' Raft Race was over and Larry Patrick, spotting a potential goldmine, was already planning some rules, revisions and entry fees for the next event.

The first affair confirmed that the majority of participants were in no hurry to complete the trip from Morgan Falls Dam to the Vinings area off route 41 Cobb Parkway and it was much more of a floating party than a race. Patrick added new prize categories for rafts, offering trophies for the best designed, and most unique showboats in commercial and non-commercial categories and downplayed the rush to the finish line. Companies large and small, inventive engineering and design students at Georgia Tech and individuals by the score began to work on their floating billboards and fantastic flotations in preparation for the next Ramblin' Raft Race.

Never missing an opportunity for more revenue, General Manager Jerry Blum loosed his gang of money-hungry sales wizards upon the top ad agencies to nail down sponsorships of the 1970 race. The metro-wide buzz of excitement and anticipation sent clear signals that the next event was going to be a big deal. Word of mouth, but mostly the on-air accounts of the first beer-soaked race by the Quixie Jocks had thousands pining over the missed opportunity to get wasted, basted, naked, stoned or seriously waterlogged and they vowed to be involved in the next so-called raft race.

I worked with Larry Patrick on the logistics for the second annual outing while being constantly reminded by the Big Three that if anything went wrong, my neck was on the line. Of course if all went smoothly, they would squabble over the credit. In other words it was typical corporate politics. Patrick dealt with the Corps of Engineers who controlled the water flow out of Morgan Falls Dam, National Park Service rangers and local police who would be responsible for traffic and crowd control.

I was swamped with paperwork and fielding phone calls. Burns called every few minutes with something else that he or Burkhart had thought of for me to do. In addition to the liability insurance the station already carried, I was ordered take out another one. Hire a plane to buzz the river all day trailing a banner saying "WQXI welcomes everyone to the raft race," have huge signs painted, flyers printed, write and produce more promos, and remember, if anything goes wrong it was my idea to get the station involved in this crazy promotion. Unless everything went well and then it was their brilliant inspiration.

Someone once said, "The Lord protects fools and drunks." Who could argue after the second race and those following for a full decade produced no fatalities or serious injuries? I doubt if any other gathering of thousands of uninhibited, alcohol-swigging party animals on rickety conveyances in a dangerous situation has ever been as fortunate as the mobs shootin' the Hooch.

The 1970 event was when it went from a race to a combination floating Mardi Gras/Woodstock on Water. There were hundreds of legitimate, blow-up rafts but also strange and ridiculous hordes of anything that would float while carrying one or more human bodies. Hundreds just floated on large inner tubes. Some tied together plastic bottles. There were old car bodies on platforms. Larry Patrick's Delta Sig brothers constructed a large, prize-worthy pirate ship which most likely would have won a trophy had it not been wrecked in the rapids. The big rocks were claiming most of the large creations which included everything but a piano. Check that, there actually was a big upright piano stranded in the rapids.

A few of the serious racers showed up with inflatable Kayaks, not technically rafts, but they had not been disqualified by the rules so they easily outdistanced everything else. No two or four person raft could compete with crafts more boat than raft. Rules were amended and categories added for the next race.

Despite gross exaggerations by gullible or devious reporters, the actual number of registered entries was right at 1,500, still a huge increase in only one year. This is not counting hundreds more who didn't enter the race officially, but jumped in somewhere along the route. The vast majority of raft race participants that year and every ensuing year consisted of spectators mobbing the bridges and lining the banks of the river.

Not only did I get involved hot and heavily with behind the scenes details, I joined the throng of beer-sotted bacchanalians in the frigid waters. A neighbor, Doug Keith was anxious to compete in the race and he talked me into joining him. Our raft was made from a huge airplane inner tube which he obtained at the Lockheed aviation plant where he worked. He added a plywood floor attaching it with rope and painting the name, USS Intrepid on the side. Several drunks misread the name as USS Inner tube during our downstream sojourn.

We arrived at what we thought would be early at the starting point just below Morgan Falls Dam. The place was packed with hundreds of tents, make-shift lean-tos and improvised shelters. Campfires burned, music blasted as revelers ran in all directions already revved up after spending the night camped out. Many huffed and puffed away with tire pumps inflating rafts. Others huffed and puffed on other substances. Larry Patrick and his crew were scrambling about attempting to organize some sort of controlled starting operation.

We brought along a 12-pack of beer and a movie camera, which were not brilliant choices for cargo as the camera got soaked ruining the film and the beer caused us to long for restroom facilities which were non-existent. Doug was serious about trying to win the race and he paddled like mad, for about ten minutes. By then, it was obvious that an inner tube with plywood floor, now half full of cold water was not about to set any speed records.

Dozens of rafts passed us, one carrying several big guys who were singing, "We don't smoke marijuana in Muskogee," as clouds of pungent smoke drifted over the USS Intrepid. Doug, who frowned on such illegal activities said, "Those guys are a disgrace," to which I muttered through chattering teeth, "Yep, way off key."

Law enforcement tended to believe the lyrics of the song also applied to the Chattahoochee. Maybe some grass, reefer, pot, weed and some joints were smoked but they were unaware of any marijuana.

It was so chilly in the river I was almost feeling sorry for the near naked girls in their bikinis and short shorts, but I got over it. Obviously our station's involvement with a Georgia Tech fraternity had produced a smash hit of monumental proportions, rife with everything our young audience loved, mostly wild debauchery.

Unwarned home owners along the banks of the river must have been startled beyond belief to suddenly witness an armada of makeshift rafts advancing on them. They undoubtedly thought that Castro had once again emptied the prisons and asylums and this time instead of Miami the Balseros were headed for Atlanta.

After a couple of hours Doug and I stopped pretending we were having a good time as we continually stepped off into the cold river to free our flimsy craft from the rocks. How any of the big monstrosities got through the rapids I will never understand. Maybe none did. A Volkswagen bug got hung up and by the time the owners rescued it a beaver had claimed squatting rights and built a home in the rear seat.

A large wooden showboat became stuck in the rapids and started coming apart, leaving jagged splinters and the ends of nails protruding to puncture several passing tubes and inflatable rafts. The slapstick never abated. By now the race had become similar to being subjected to a three-and-a-half hour version of Thelma and Louise, where I keep asking myself, "Is this thing ever going to end?"

At last we staggered ashore, slipping, sliding and crawling up the muddy banks dragging the now hated USS Intrepid, to mingle with the crowd of exhausted, sun burnt, soaking-wet raft race victims. I couldn't help but notice several tons of discarded plywood, tubes, coolers, cans, bottles, blankets and clothing. A quite unsightly collection of trash, I mused, wonder who'll have to clean it up? Don't ask.

My clever scheme to air announcements inviting our fun-loving raft racers to join us for a clean-up party and offering nice prizes for most junk collected brought out a throng of about four people. Fraternity members, the DJs, a couple of ladies from the station and I cleaned up the Vinings landing area. As far as I was concerned hauling trash was more fun than shootin' the Hootch.

Nobody asked my opinion. The next year, the Chattahoochee Ramblin' Raft Race had at least twice as many active participants with crowds of spectators estimated at 300,000. Typical moronic printed reports claimed 300,000 rafts, which would be impossible unless the river was packed from Morgan Falls Dam for a hundred miles to Columbus, Georgia. Here's a tip. If you ever need a big crowd estimate, get a quote from the spokesperson for the police department in charge of traffic and crowd control. You will not be disappointed.

Larry Patrick soon formed the American Rafting Association, securing all rights to the Ramblin' Raft Race. He sold the promotion to several radio stations all over the Eastern and Midwestern United States sending in his crew to take care of the myriad details and legwork. It was a radio promotion all the way and one of the best ever. Someone should have informed a few ace reporters that it did not spring from spontaneous combustion but was the result of a radio station working in cooperation with a brilliant young man from Georgia Tech.

The third annual race was a replay of the second with more entrants and observers. By 1971 it was national and international news with CBS TV mentioning it on the evening news, a French documentary was produced and a full-length movie, The Great Raft Race was released based on the '71 affair.

Governor Jimmy Carter declared the race route The Chattahoochee River National Recreation Area. We weren't dealing with peanuts. Eventually 10 other waterways were also named National Recreation areas due to the Ramblin' Raft Races.

As a token of my appreciation and as an excuse for a party, Dixie and I invited all the DJs, Larry Patrick and his crew and all WQXI staffers to our farm for a cookout on the evening of the race. Station management gave us permission to purchase a whole pig to barbecue. A part time Jock, Dave Weiss picked it up from the butcher shop. Our plans to present the prepared porker with an apple in his mouth were thwarted when Dave ordered the butcher to remove the pig's head because he couldn't stand the way it was staring at him. When he brought it to our place the evening prior to the race, it was obviously much too big to fit into the refrigerator. We packed it in a bathtub full of ice. And so to bed. Tomorrow would be a long, busy day.

Sometime during the night our six year old daughter awoke and called for her mother. Dixie stumbled into the bathroom still half asleep after tending to the kid and snapped on the light. She emitted a blood-curdling scream at the sight of the stark-white, bloody body in the bathtub. I had neglected to inform her where Dave and I had stowed the pig.

Dixie's mother, Pauline Pelkey was up at dawn, happy as could be for the chance to barbecue a whole pig. We dug a grave-size hole and put flat daybed springs over it as a grill. Pauline basted and seasoned the pork for twelve hours and by party time it was tender, falling off the bone delicious. Guests talked about the fun party for years. It took place in a freshly mowed horse pasture next to an old, abandoned farmhouse under the trees on a gorgeous evening in late May.

One of the attendees was a young lady in a small bikini. She was representing one of the race's sponsors, Aztec Tanning Lotion. Miss Aztec was tanned a dark bronze from head to toe. Knowing what we now know about harmful rays from the sun, I suspect the former beauty queen has more wrinkles than a corduroy leisure suit.

The laughing, eating and drinking was still going on when I gave up and went to bed at four A M. Especially the drinking. Dixie and I moped out to clean up the leftovers the next day. There were none. Every morsel of the pig, five gallons of Brunswick stew and several cases of beer and soft drinks had all disappeared. Raft race involvement is evidently a fine appetizer. Now we know where the expression pigging out comes from.

TEN

Turn the Beat Around

By the time I joined WQXI in 1969 it was a highly rated, nationally respected Top 40 operation, winning big ratings due to the programming expertise of Kent Burkhart, and a top money maker under the leadership of Jerry Blum, most likely the best media salesperson in America and mentor to radio Account Executives. Unlike most General Managers I have known Jerry dared to spend large amounts of money to make larger amounts.

Shortly after I arrived, the station sponsored a city-wide scavenger/treasure hunt for invited clients and ad agency people, awarding prizes of appliances and other high-ticket items including a pair of new sports cars. It's no mystery why WQXI received millions in extra time buys. Under Jerry's tutelage, Clark Brown and Mark Kanov rose through the ranks from Account Execs to General Managers and even higher in the corporate hierarchy. Mike Dana preferred to remain in sales and was extremely effective as one of the top-billing time salesmen in America. My closest friend in the Sales Department was Clay Sledge, a former DJ who also shared my passion for horses.

This crew of pranksters was not known as anything but Salesmen prior to political correctness and the hiring of females to sell commercial time. The first lady in that capacity at WQXI was Beth Smith and she quickly brought in business second only to super salesman Mike Dana. The sales guys loved to razz and play practical jokes on one another when they were not counting their money, modeling fancy clothes or making fun of the Disc Jockeys. The sales staff had trade out deals, meaning the station ran free commercials for clothiers and sales and management got free wardrobes. This enabled the sharply dressed account execs to sneer and insult everyone else's clothes. A couple of them were also car crazy.

While watching a TV show about custom cars and their smitten owners, I asked Dixie, "How can anyone fall in love with an inanimate object?"

She pondered for a moment then replied, "I must have had a reason."

Ignoring her feeble, amateurish attempt at humor, I began to mentally review The Great Corvette Caper, an actual case from the files of my head wherein a friend and co-worker drove himself to a near nervous breakdown. Only the names have been changed to protect the guilty and possibly prevent a vengeful retaliation even at this late date.

You've probably known others like Clyde, a person so enamored of his vehicle he would never dream of parking it without getting out and circling it several times, admiring his wonderful ride from various angles, his grinning mug resembling a proud parent peering through a maternity ward window. as it is reflected in the daily wash job. Parking places for such beloved buggies are not hastily chosen.

As is customary with his ilk, Clyde often spent an hour or more searching for a spot with adjoining empty spaces, allowing him to hog at least two spots to protect his Stingray's finish from swinging doors. Such king-sized spaces often meant a long hike, but were the only alternative to German Sheppard watch dogs and armed guards. Clyde, though a fickle car lover who traded them in promiscuously, would have no sooner left his beloved silver Corvette in a regular parking space than abandon it on a dark street in South Chicago.

Incidentally, car fanatics do not have paint jobs on their chariots. They have finishes. They don't have headlights, but high and low beams. In the interest of brevity, they have a special title for every part down to the final screw. Never are they heard to mutter a brand or model name. They smugly refer to their mobile treasures as an "SS, 104, BL T, X n O, or I 812," in some elite code, ever hoping that someone will overhear them and ask for more details.

Deep car infatuation may be somewhat excusable in certain circumstances, such as a teenager's first automobile, or for any owner whose mode of transportation cost more than a five-bedroom McMansion in a gated community, but most authorities agree that eroticism should rarely involve two-thousand pound metal objects after males voices have changed.

Clyde had devised a system to foil thoughtless and ill-mannered owners of inferior vehicles. He confiscated a "Reserved For Customers Only" parking space owned by a bank which was located below the radio station's second floor offices. Although Clyde had no account there, he justified his use of the space by strolling into the bank once in a while and asking the teller if she could give him change for a five.

Nowadays I shudder in recalling how a fairly handsome, Corvette-loving, nattily-attired Account Executive soon came to resemble a disheveled, rapidly balding, aged wastrel, more likely the possessor of a dilapidated jalopy on blocks in a weed-filled yard than a high-powered chick magnet. So sad.

Whenever Clyde had to leave his car it evoked images of teary-eyed lovers in old movies, parting as the hero heads off to an undetermined fate. Between incoming calls from clients begging to buy airtime on the only Top 40 station in the city, Clyde sat at his desk thumbing through colorful brochures of the latest S.S, LOLs, BLTs, OMGs etc. while fondling his keys.

Such serious love affairs spark jealousy and his ornery cohorts soon hatched a sabotage plot. They listened with feigned interest to his rambling praise for the automobile, even encouraging him at times. Finally one prankster asked Clyde if he could drive the precious car around the block just to confirm that it was as magnificent as Clyde claimed. After prolonged plotter pressure, Clyde reluctantly handed over the keys, as anxious as any father watching his teenage daughter leave on her first date with a tattooed motorcyclist.

The villain sped around the block and then to the nearest General Motors dealer to have a set of duplicate keys made. The Corvette was returned unscathed to the great relief of a nervous Clyde who had no inkling that the trap was baited and set.

After lunch the following day, Clyde sat at his desk with a worried look on his face. Finally he broke the silence in the large office that he shared with four other sales people, announcing "Somebody got in my car and turned it around it its parking space." The strange news was greeted with total apathy.

The following afternoon, Clyde muttered to the sales staff, "I'm either losing my mind or somebody's messing around with my car." This time one of the guys asked him to explain himself.

"The last two days when I went back to my car, it was facing the opposite direction from where I parked it."

Everyone scoffed, snickered and derided Clyde, accusing him of being drunk, senile, stupid, addled or most likely lying. No one seemed to notice that one man left the room during the chatter.

"I saw your Corvette parked in that reserved bank spot when I came in," said someone.

"Which way was it facing," inquired Clyde.

"North, toward the car lot next door."

"Yeah, that's how I parked it, but I wouldn't be surprised if some jerk doesn't turn it around again."

"Well, we think you're pulling our legs, but c'mon., let's go look."

The pair took the elevator downstairs, walked outside and saw that the car was parked exactly as Clyde had left it. By the time they got back upstairs it was turned around facing south toward the Morrison's Cafeteria.

When Clyde left the office later that afternoon and spotted his turned-around car, he sprinted back upstairs.

"Alright, take a look now, it's happened again," he panted.

Looking bored, a couple of the guys went back downstairs with Clyde and naturally the car had been turned around and was again facing north in its original position.

A quite concerned salesman asked, "Are you okay Clyde? Have you been under pressure?"

"I swear, five minutes ago," he mumbled, it was, it…" Shuffling off he got into his Stingray and drove out of the lot, weaving.

As the days went by, Clyde's appearance began to deteriorate. His snappy ensembles became rumpled and as dispirited as his face. His pale cheeks were often covered with gray stubble, his sparse hair uncombed. His hands trembled, his voice quivered. Coworkers ignored him and never commented on his appearance or asked about his car. Meanwhile, using the duplicate keys, they continued to turn his car around every time they got a chance.

Clyde began to hide in the small, cramped space behind the passenger seat, lurking in wait for the fiend who was tampering with his illegally parked car. In the stifling Georgia summer heat he waited in vain, hour after hour and day after day as sweat poured from him, drenching his expensive shirts and coats. Occasionally from a window on the second floor one of his snickering colleagues would spot his damp head as it bobbed up as his bloodshot eyes quickly scanned the area then disappeared back into the virtual oven.

The middle-aged lady who managed the bank finally took notice and called the police to report a peeping Tom who was obviously in cahoots with a group of weirdoes who hung out in the building, and who kept turning their getaway car around several times a day in preparation for a bank heist.

Following a long conference involving the entire sales staff, the FBI, the bank Manager, and Clyde's psychiatrist, the Silver Corvette stopped turning itself around and Clyde started parking in two spots on the far, upper deck of the lot.

No one ever confessed, but soon a set of Corvette keys mysteriously appeared on Clyde's desk. They were traded in with the rest of the flashy car for a sedate Buick. The Corvette was a soiled mistress. It was a cruel prank, as is any really good practical joke.

Being a careful, neutral observer, I filed the trick away and attempted to pull it on a pompous boss several years later. I obtained an impression of his keys, had extras made and turned his parked car around every day for a week. He never noticed.

Louie Louie
Say What?

WQXI's call letters had been selected in the early 60s by former owner Bill Lowery and nicknamed Quixie to produce the rhyming phrase "Quixie in Dixie." Following a successful radio career, Bill Lowery moved on to achieve even greater success in the music recording and publishing business, with such artists as Billy Joe Royal, Jerry Reed, Ray Stevens, Tommy Roe, Joe South, Dennis Yost and The Classics Four, The Atlanta Rhythm Section, and the list goes on.

Pacific and Southern Broadcasting owned stations in Denver, Portland, Cincinnati, Denver, and later Hackensack/NYC, in addition to Atlanta. Kent Burkhart was a VP in charge of all programming working closely with George Burns, the National Program Director who supervised each station's Program Director including yours truly at the bottom of the chain of command. I assume everyone realizes that I am not referring to the ancient comedian when I refer to George Burns, though I have known him to loudly utter the phrase, "Oh God," usually over something one of the DJs had done.

WQXI also had a Music Director, Sylvia Clark who met with record promoters, fielded their constant phone calls and weeded out the few potential hits from the hundred or more new records that arrived weekly. Most records that make a major market playlist have been around a few weeks and have already been tested on smaller market stations. Programmers also have access to several trade publications that track the progress or decline of records which takes a lot of guesswork out of adding and dropping music selections. I met with Sylvia each week and she asked for my opinion of potential adds but all final decisions had to be approved by Kent Burkhart. He had built WQXI into one of the most coveted stations in America for record adds. Obviously his music decisions were not to be disputed.

Vice President Spiro Agnew, speaking for the Nixon administration before he was forced to resign from office for a series of high crimes and misdemeanors, made a speech attacking rock and roll music and radio stations that play it, hinting that the FCC might be revoking the licenses of broadcast facilities that were leading American youths down the path to destruction. Word came down from Burkhart via Burns that I was responsible for all lyrical content aired on Quixie. At least I was in charge of something. The brass had informed the record companies that they had to submit printed copies of every record's lyrics before it would be considered for air play and they flat out refused. I did not have that option. Before a record went on the air, I had to listen to it and transcribe the lyrics with copies to the programming decision makers. It was possibly the worst radio-related chore I ever had to perform.

Listening over and over to mush-mouthed, mumbling and screaming of nonsensical gibberish and trying to get the words on paper was a nightmare. Talk about obscenities. I'm glad no one recorded me. Patience, I told myself, there are only a few new records added each week. Then I got the order to review every record already on the air including the library of oldies. Spiro could be listening. Any record that might be interpreted as condoning sex or drugs was to be banned from our pure as virgin olive oil airwaves. It was a happy day for me and the record promoters after a few weeks when someone in the ivory tower decided that the Whitehouse heat had abated and that we were missing out on too many million-selling hits, therefore the lyric transcribing ended.

My duties under the multi-layer of bosses consisted of baby-sitting the DJs, filling out mounds of paperwork and occasionally pulling an air shift for a hung-over or vacationing Jock. WQXI was the flagship station for the Atlanta Falcons football network and after several distracted or disinterested board operators had messed up the network broadcasts by missing cues, I took over running the console myself as our Sports Director Jack Hurst called the play by play. My credo has always been no job too big, no job too small, which could be phrased as the familiar, "If you want something done right, do it yourself," even if it's a pain in the neck, is an unpaid chore and ruins your weekend.

As another hedge against one of Nixon's henchman showing up any day with a wrecking crew to dismantle our anti-American, morals destroying pop music station, the big brass decided to assign all department heads to seek out and conduct face to face interviews with community leaders to ascertain their opinions on how WQXI could best serve the needs of the public. Our Community affairs Director, Maureen Roberts complied a huge list of prospects for us to phone and schedule appointments for interviews.

I met with the State Superintendent of Schools, several politicians and self-appointed leaders but soon, I was looking at long drives to small towns far from the city. Mike Dana, Sales Manager at the time and I teamed up and headed out for the boondocks. We were sometimes welcomed and sometimes met with suspicious glares, suspected of being big town radio trouble makers who were trying to dig up dirt for an expose. Most of the time no real official would talk to us so we would interview a store owner, the local postmaster or a loafer on a park bench, making up an impressive title for him in our report. The Police in Douglasville, Georgia threatened us with jail time for barging in without an appointment and we decided to start faking the in-person interviews and make use of the telephones.

Before long I turned it into a joke, phoning and interviewing such community leaders as a combination preacher/tattoo removal specialist and a mule dealer. No one in the company complained, which proved to me that none of our reports were being read by anyone.

ELEVEN

There's Something Happening Here

After running virtually unopposed in pop hit radio for several years WQXI faced an alleged challenge in the early 70s from WIIN, a daytime only outlet. Jim Davenport, owner and General Manager of WFOM, Marietta had been programming Adult Contemporary music on his low-powered suburban station for some time and while it had been recognized as one of the best small market stations in America, it posed little threat in the metro market with its piss ant signal.

Davenport, without question the most colorful and unique person to ever manage a radio station or promote records was known to grab a deer rifle during a night of partying in the studios and shoot out the red warning lights on the station's broadcast tower. The fact that it cost hundreds of dollars for a specialist to scale hundreds of feet up the antenna to replace the huge bulbs was of no concern as long as it added to the Ol' Bear legend.

All the local record pluggers gathered at WFOM Monday evenings to pitch their products. A nice, civil, democratic method of voting would decide which new records would be added to the playlist. In case of ties or borderline records being hyped by two or more reps, Davenport would bring out the boxing gloves and the gang would venture outside to witness the competitors as they beat one other senseless. The winner would have his record awarded a coveted position on the WFOM playlist. The loser, well, all he could do was hope for a smaller opponent next Monday evening.

The term Adult Contemporary or AC had replaced the old Top 40 tag and was a more accurate term for pop radio since very few stations actually played forty current records. They were much more likely to play thirty or fewer legitimate hits along with a few oldies. Programmers consider it an unspeakable horror to be caught playing a stiff. Any record that does not crack the top thirty and stay there for a few weeks is not a bomb, nor a flop nor a dud. It's worse. In radio lingo it is known as a stiff, something as dead as the rotting corpse to which the term was first applied. Stiffs cause fickle listeners to tune out, perhaps to put up with static and interference on WFOM or the upstart WIIN. Therefore judicious care was practiced in the selection of the few new records added to a play list each week.

Since I was certainly not to be trusted with new record adds, Music

Director Sylvia Clark weeded out the stiffs by staying informed with the fate of new releases in smaller markets, tracking them in the trades, calling local record stores and eliminating stiffs by the score, much to the chagrin of record promoters who were thoroughly convinced that radio stations should add every record released and who would never be satisfied with anything less. Sylvia then talked to Burns and Burkhart, made her recommendations and explained the reasoning behind her choices. Burkhart had the final say, which was good news for R & B hits, bad news for almost anything sounding Country. What Burkhart didn't like Sylvia and George didn't like. I was given leeway to mess with the oldies library and just to see how long it would be before one of them demanded we get rid of it, I would occasionally sneak in an old Johnny Cash or Buck Owens song.

George Burns called me several times to discuss the WIIN menace, asking me what I planned to do about it. Upper level programming was concerned that they would carve out a significant chunk of our audience, but I considered them of little consequence. Insufficient paranoia was to be my downfall as a Program Director.

In the old Mel Brooks movie, High Anxiety, he plays a shrink in an Institution for the Very,Very Nervous. I firmly believe such a facility is sorely needed in real life after working under a few programmers who existed in a constant state of terror. I always figured, correctly, than if I was fired from a job I could get another one.

A bigger concern than another AM station was WPLO FM, programmed by former WQXI newsman, Ed Shane. The FM band was finally beginning to make a move as WPLO FM came on with an automated, album-oriented format and practically no talk. Atlanta was still in the midst of the Hippie era and album cuts were considered far superior to un-cool 45 singles according to the long-haired Peacenik wannabes. To that crowd our hits were sneeringly dismissed as childish bubblegum while even the most insufferable album cut was groovy beyond measure.

Kent Burkhart was notorious for hiring the best people away from perceived competition and moving them out of the market. Ed Shane was hired to join our company and was made Program Director of KKDJ in Los Angeles. Asked about his early LP format later, he said, "Success killed it. The more popular it became the less exclusive it seemed." Underground radio was not long in coming up into the sunshine and the obscure album cuts were gradually replaced with legitimate hits.

I'm Walkin' the Floor Over You

The company had moved their programming President and VP from Atlanta to Denver by 1971 and I was asked to fly out for a meeting. Dixie and I considered it a welcome mini-vacation. We stayed with George Burns and his family and enjoyed touring a horse farm, the Pike's Peak area and an old silver mining ghost town turned tourist attraction. The scenery was gorgeous and I thoroughly enjoyed our visit except for George's constant worried look and nervous pacing. I attended a genial meeting in their offices as we discussed programming philosophies and creative ideas while Dixie was treated to a great lunch and a tour of the Mile High City with Sylvia Clark and Mrs. Burns. It seemed like a long way to travel and a lot of company expense for nothing but a friendly chat but a small vacation for me and my wife was a nice perk.

When it was time to leave we took a cab to the airport. We were pleasantly surprised to encounter Ike and Tina Turner walking through the terminal, but before we could talk about it a typically garbled announcement crackled over the loudspeakers, "Gary Corry, phone call for Gary Corry." I took the call at the nearest airline counter. It was from George Burns who asked me if I would I be willing to remain at WQXI as the morning DJ, or would I prefer to be do the morning show on their recently acquired New York City market station, if the company made a change of Program Directors. I was somewhat surprised but not shocked. I had already lasted much longer than most WQXI Program Directors. I told him that I would make a choice after talking it over with Dixie when we got back to Atlanta. George was always good at communicating by phone.

My choices were to stay in Atlanta and work for new Program Director Bill Sherard, a guy with a hard-nosed reputation who was expected to clean house by firing all the DJs, or I could move to The Big Apple for triple the salary I was making. I chose the money, the chance to be back on the air and the exciting adventure of working in the Nation's largest market.

The Program Director at WWDJ was Nick Anthony, whom I had worked for during the Bill Drake consulting era at WUBE. I had recommended him for the PD job at WSAI and he was transferred to WWDJ when the company bought the facility. The station had formerly been a Country outlet with the call letters WJRZ. I would also be reunited with old friend Bwana Johnny, the afternoon Jock.

WQXI gave me a going-away party and most of the on-air and office employees turned out to bid me and my family farewell. I was presented with a surprise gift of a saddle which really wasn't much of a surprise because Clay Sledge, the designated shopper had taken me along to pick the one I wanted. The ever-thoughtful programming department in Denver gave me a whole week to get to New Jersey and find a place for me, Dixie, our three kids, two dogs and fourteen horses. No problem. I stayed with Bwana, searched for a farm to lease during the day and got acquainted with the notorious New York City rudeness at night.

Dining in restaurants was an experience quite unlike a trip to a Southern Waffle House where the waitresses smile and call everyone Honey or Darling. New York waiters treated customers as unwelcome pests and intruders, but the food they grudgingly slammed down on the tables was pretty good. Naturally, Bwana and I did everything we could to further irritate surly wait staff. We always brought out mischievous pranks in one another, much to the frustration of waiters, clerks and several Program Directors.

By some miracle and with the help of a big money reward to a retired Coast Guard officer turned real estate salesman, I snared a 250 acre horse farm for lease just in time to avoid being sent back home to Atlanta and a precarious DJ job.

While others around me tend to worry and fret when a major move looms, I am able to remain fairly calm and confident, knowing that The Lord will put us where he wants us to be. He wanted us to experience a few years in northern New Jersey and it was a wonderful time in my life as I competed for the New York radio ratings in the early morning hours, then spent afternoons and evenings with my family on a big farm nestled in the wooded hills with a trout-stocked lake, green pastures and a couple of barns full of horses.

My home life caused resentment among the staff back in Hackensack. They lived in small houses or apartments and gathered on afternoons and evenings to drink and talk about records, formats, promotions and their dreams of being number one. Radio was their lives. Radio was my way of making enough money to support my family and allow us to live in the country and raise horses.

I Feel, I Feel, I Feel Like A Morning Star

After a few days on the air using my real name, the one that had served me well for eleven years on the air, Burkhart decided I had to change it. Gary Corry was not good enough for New York. I thought it was a weird idea since hundreds of thousands of listeners had been subjected to my name every few minutes, but Corry had to go. This was just before Hollywood and millions of parents decided to start naming kids of either sex Corey, Cory, Correy or Kori. Burkhart preferred Robin Scott, which caused me to nearly puke. I am no more a Robin Scott than I am a Fauntleroy Terwillinger. It just doesn't fit. I agreed to use my middle name and a grudging acquiescence came back from Denver. I went from being Gary Corry for 36 years to Gary Russell in one day.

The studios of WWDJ, hereafter referred to as 97 DJ since north easterners didn't boycott radio stations with less than three call letters as Cincinnati natives tended to do, were a disappointment. From a fancy office amidst modern studios located in an upscale building in the prestigious Buckhead area on world famous Peachtree Street in Atlanta to an old house on a side street in Hackensack was not the upward move to a luxurious urban setting I had imagined. While on the air, I could turn around and look out the back door to watch squirrels playing in the trees next to a small creek that flowed by the building. This is the most exciting metropolitan market in America?

In the early days of 97 DJ, unionized broadcast engineers were involved in a somewhat strange manner. The Jocks could cue up and start the records and cassette tapes but an engineer sat at a table about ten feet away on the other side of a studio window controlling the volume and the microphone switch. I had always thought that it would be just great to have an engineer running the console for me while I relaxed and dreamed up my next clever quip. The 97 DJ procedures were almost as frustrating as the frantic routine I went through at WRAJ. The engineers tended to be rather disinterested in my hilarious ad libs and the wonderful hit music. They liked reading newspapers, working crossword puzzles or chatting on the phone while I waved frantically for someone to turn on my microphone or to turn the volume up on turntable two. After each slight deviation in our slam-bang format, the hotline would ring and the Program Director would ask the question to which he knew the answer, "What happened?"

I would let out a long sigh and explain that the engineer was late in reacting and he would tell me to get on his case, chew him out. Right. That would have immediately resulted in a complaint being filed with their union and guess who would have received the blame for causing trouble? After a couple of months their union agreed to allow the DJs to operate all their own knobs and switches. Thereafter the engineers mostly just sat around killing time, drinking coffee, reading and talking about how they missed the old Country music format that was in place prior to our seizing control with Donny Osmond records.

The Gotham City market was a long way from Atlanta or Cincinnati but several of my friends and former co-workers were around to make me feel right at home. Bwana Johnny, Nick Anthony, Al Law Brady, and Steve Clark had all been part of WCPO or WUBE and good friend Mike Dineen was doing mornings at WXLO FM across the bridge in New York City.

The initial Disc Jockey staff at 97 DJ consisted of me, Mike Phillips, Bill Bailey, Bwana, Ronnie Grant and lone holdover from the Country station, all-night Jock Bob Lockwood. Naturally many DJs passed through the proverbial swinging doors in the next three years. I was late arriving for my shift one morning due to an alarm clock malfunction and Lockwood seized the opportunity to display his repertoire of impressions and witticisms. The end result was his being fired because up until then the Program Director said he never realized how bad he was.

We rocked and rolled our little hearts out giving away T-shirts, albums, money and trips to far off dens of inequity, striving to compete with FM stations but mostly the extremely powerful WABC. 97 DJ had a pretty strong signal with 5,000 watts full-time. However it was in a directional pattern and we had a huge territory to cover in the metro area. WABC boomed out 50,000 watts from Maine to Florida making our signal sound like the speakers at a McDonald's drive through.

Perhaps as a harbinger of things to come, the sales department set up a promotion with legendary Jets quarterback Joe Namath. I was to call Broadway Joe each morning and do a bit with him on the air. Every time I phoned there was a long series of rings before Joe finally mumbled, "Hello." I would remind him who I was and why I was calling to which he would inevitably say, "Oh, call me back after 'while, Man," and hang up. "After 'while," the show was over. I was never once able to put Joe on the air.

Everything we tried to do was a challenge due to red tape, regulations and union rules. The station had a so-called Magic Bus with a garish, psychedelic paint job that the Jocks and other station employees drove around handing out trinkets and phoning in reports. The van was required to have a commercial license tag and that prevented it from using the Jersey Turnpike. We could only get to selected communities without a long, winding detour.

Despite our problems the station was making a big splash in the market. At our peak Nick Anthony invited me into his office to see the results of the latest Pulse ratings. He pointed out that although I was a ways behind the morning Jock at WABC, Harry Harrison, I had more listeners than any other Adult Contemporary DJ in America, more than the top DJs in Chicago, Los Angeles or San Francisco. That was nice, but the problem was WABC and Harry Harrison who we were never going to beat because we couldn't even reach a huge chunk of his audience with our signal. Since advertising agencies are seldom interested in buying time on also-runs, 97 DJ was bleeding money like Fannie Mae.

New Year's Weekend 1974 Anthony invited me back into his office to fire me. Despite my good ratings he explained that the company wanted to go in another direction, which is a standard weasel line. The new Jock imported from Philadelphia quickly lost about half the listeners I had attracted. I received a nice severance check and went home to run our horse business and contemplate my options. After three years in the market I had not made contact with other station personnel other than Mike Dineen so I wasn't in a position to pick up the phone and ask any programmer pal for a job.

I bought a mimeograph machine and started a DJ comedy service which kept me occupied for a while but certainly didn't put me into a higher income tax bracket. I got a lot of mail from nomadic Jocks saying such things as, "Send me the stuff and if I like it, I'll send you a check." Now that's comedy.

A few weeks after I was canned, I received a phone call from the 97 DJ News Director Steve Hollis. He asked me if I was interested in doing newscasts on a per diem basis. I had read the news on my shows at WRAJ, WIBV, WCPO and WUBE so yes, I would be happy to read news copy aloud for the per diem union rate. It's a fancy pants Latin term for part-time, and thanks to the AFTRA union it required stations to pay at a higher daily rate than the full-timers contracts. This was to prevent stations from running their operations with a bunch of part-timers, a common practice now for cheapskates in non-union markers who do not want to provide their lowly announcers with any benefits. A per diem announcer in the New York market could work three or four days a week and make as much as a full time DJ or news reporter. Sometimes things that don't make sense make a lot of sense.

With all the hungry news readers in the New York, New Jersey area there was only one reason for the News Director to offer me, an out of work Disc Jockey the job. The Rolling Stones had performed at Madison Square Garden and we DJs had received VIP tickets. I am not fond of concerts to put it mildly and did not plan to attend. The Garden is a long way from extreme Northwest Jersey where I lived and I had no desire to be driving nearly a hundred miles home only to rise at four A M and head back to work.

I could have sold the tickets for a goodly amount, but Steve Hollis approached me and asked if there was any way possible to find tickets to the sold-out show. His daughter was a diehard Stones fan and he promised her he would try to find tickets, but figured it to be an impossible task. He couldn't believe it when I said, "I've got two you can have." I refused to accept payment for them and truthfully told him that being able to make him and his daughter happy was my reward. I have a daughter too, so I could relate. He told me later that his daughter thought her father was the greatest hero in the world and he would never forget what I did. He kept his word. Steve was a good man who ran an efficient news operation. He got around in a wheelchair or on crutches after a mentally ill, unqualified character who applied for a job shot him upon being told that his application would be kept on file.

Soon after I started filling in for news people at 97 DJ I received a call from the Program Director of WPAT, a successful adult music station and was soon doing news on both stations. I also pulled shifts occasionally on WPAT FM as an announcer-DJ if one can call changing twenty minute long music tapes jocking discs. I had been recommended by Steve Hollis.

Nick Anthony left the company and Al Law Brady took over as Program Director. He phoned and offered me a per diem DJ job. I then began juggling three part-time gigs, sometimes making the fifty mile drive home to grab an hour or two of rest then heading back to the other station while my car seat was still warm.

The New York, New Jersey audience was not much different than the listeners in Cincinnati or Atlanta from my perspective with a few exceptions. I had a regular caller named John who liked to chat about sports .He was a die-hard Yankee fan in his thirties who hated the Mets and all their fans, and it seemed that the Mets fans felt the same about the Yankees and their followers. Surprisingly, he admitted that he had never been to a Yankees game. When I asked him about some of the city's famous landmarks such as the Statue of Liberty, he told me that he, as most of his Brooklyn acquaintances never ventured more than a couple of blocks from their homes. He said that he would feel threatened and out of place away from familiar territory and had spent his entire life within walking distance of his apartment. No place like home.

Recurring nightmares are not unique among radio people. Who hasn't dreamed of being in school, unprepared for a test or being far from class when a test is scheduled? Mine is worse and it's based on a true incident. I wake in a sweat coming out of a dream where I am on the air in an obscure radio station, frantically searching for records, tape cartridges, CDs or news copy while the unforgivable sin of dead air makes a hissing sound and a red light flashes on and off signaling a hotline call from a furious boss.

I don't need a shrink to help me find the cause of my nightmare. One night I sped from WPAT to 97-DJ barely in time to begin the midnight to 6 AM shift by reading a 15 minute newscast. I discovered that the departing newshound had rather thoughtlessly or deliberately cleared the news wires and thrown out all the copy except a few headlines and some farm news. Perhaps it was a practical joke on the former number two most listened to rock DJ turned part time fill-in newscaster. If he hasn't passed on from old age, I'll get him back as soon as I think of something as heartless as his prank.

Reading slowly and redundantly, I went on the air trying to kill time. As I sweated my way through the news the hotline bulb flashed constantly even though the genius calling must have realized I was in no position to chat.

As luck would have it our latest Program Director by default was awake and listening and after I had read the headlines three or four times and informed the New York City metro area listeners of the latest hog prices and other vital farm news, I started the music, picked up the phone and explained that I was not drunk, stoned, dying or suffering from a complete mental breakdown. My explanation of the missing news copy did nothing to endear me to him, but since he was one of the DJs I once used as the butt of jokes I doubt if anything short of my dropping dead would have satisfied him. Now I'll probably have that rotten dream again tonight.

Around four A M one morning while I was filling in on 97 DJ, I received a phone call from Mel Phillips, Program Director of WXLO FM, the station where my friend Mike Dineen was working. They were looking for a Disc Jockey and Mike had recommended me. Mel was listening, acted as if he liked my style, and invited me to come to his office for an interview two days later. I expected to be nailing down a full-time job just across the George Washington Bridge in legendary Manhattan.

To make sure I wasn't late for my two o'clock appointment, I left home a couple of hours early. There might be some traffic in the city. There was. The studios were right in the heart of the sleazy Broadway and 42nd street honking, cussing, threatening pandemonium and it took an hour and a half to drive around the block to a parking garage where they charged me about a week's pay. I got to the disappointingly drab offices, checked in with the receptionist and sat down to wait. After several minutes the receptionist answered an in-station buzz, listened, and asked me, "What was it you wanted to see Mr. Phillips about?"

I repeated, "I have an appointment with him to talk about a job." She relayed the message and I waited again. Finally a guy walked out, frowned, and asked me why we were supposed to have an appointment. I reminded him of his phone call. We went into his office for a brief chat and he dismissed me, saying he would let me know. That was the last I heard from him. He had forgotten about calling me and our appointment, which was okay, since I had already decided that I wanted no part of wonderful, magical Times Square. Mike told me later that Phillips said he had thought I was a younger guy, not some old geezer in his thirties. Such are the workings of radio brains.

Papa Don't Preach

By 1974 WWDJ was on its last legs, having tried in vain with multiple changes in management, programming and DJs with ever decreasing ratings. The numbers they had before they decided to make some changes were the best they would ever achieve. I hadn't been working the all-night shift because they were signing off at midnight leaving "the city that never sleeps" with only one AM rocker after the bewitching hour. The 70s were the beginning of the end even for the mighty WABC as an AC station. Young people had turned on to the FM stations in a big way and even when they did listen to AM radio it was not cool to admit it.

The company fired all of the office personnel and air staff by March except the Program Director whom they played for a sap, implying that they were planning to retain him under a new format. They put him to work transferring religious music onto tape reels. When they had enough recorded to play between sold program slots he was fired. They got rid of all their equipment and moved the operation from the semi-lovely old house to a metal building at the transmitter site across the street.

97 DJ had lasted almost three years as a rock and roll station with a huge audience, but somehow the sales department was never able to keep up their end of the operation and finally upper management pulled the plug.

The fickle finger of fate had me on the air to utter the last words and play the last song ever heard on the 97 DJ rock format. A sore throat had me sounding a little hoarse as I hit the button to start Suite Judy Blue Eyes shortly before midnight on March 31, 1974. My last ad lib was, "I'm losing my voice, which is okay, 'cause I'm out of work," then instantly Crosby, Stills and Nash, sang, "It's getting to the point where I don't care anymore..."

Most listeners thought it was just one more crazy DJ, April fool prank, announcing that the station was switching to all inspirational programming. The big brass had finally made the right decision. There were countless churches and religious organizations clamoring to purchase air time in the New York City market to beg for donations and the station with a skeleton crew of engineers and one announcer/manager started turning a profit overnight. I'm glad someone did.

TWELVE

Going Back To Georgia

WPAT hadn't been begging for my services and anyone who believes he can make a living in the horse business is a self-deluded idiot to put it nicely. I decided that I would rather be out of work in Georgia than out of work in The Icebox, which is the term used to accurately describe northwest New Jersey.

Dixie's mother Pauline located a 48 acre farm in Georgia that we could afford and we made plans to move there sight unseen. We purchased a big truck that was used to transport horses and I began to haul our horses and furniture a thousand miles southward. On the first of three excruciating trips, Mike Dineen volunteered to ride along with me. I'm not sure which was the biggest "trip," the long drive or my traveling companion.

"Give me a cigarette, but I just quit smoking, so don't let me have one every time I ask. Just give me one when I really want one."

That was a typical Dineen statement, just the kind of twisted logic that causes confusion, misunderstandings, divorces and wars. I gave him a cigarette and asked, "How am I to know when you really want one?"

"I can't believe you'd ask such a dumb question," he replied. "You people who smoke do it out of habit and most of the time you don't even really want one. Non-smokers like me only smoke when we really want one."

Maybe he was right. Smoking is not sensible. Neither of us smoke now and I wish we had stopped sooner. After what seemed only a few minutes he asked for another cigarette.

"Is this one of the times you want one?"

"Yes it is."

He continued to bum cigarettes every half-hour or so until I finally lost patience and snapped, "Forget it. You're smoking more than I am and according to you, you're a non-smoker."

"Well, there's nothing else to do and your driving makes me nervous."

"What's wrong with the way I drive?"

"For one thing you're driving ahead of your lights."

"How do you drive ahead of your lights," I asked.

"If you see something in the road, by the time your lights hit it, you couldn't stop in time."

"I'm only going fifty miles an hour," I said. "If I drive any slower it'll take a week to get there. These horses are tired, hot, thirsty, hungry and mad like me. Only thing they don't want is my last cigarette."

"Let me have one," he demanded.

"This is not one of the times."

"Yes it is."

"No it ain't."

"How would you know? This is definitely one of the times I really want one."

"If I can't tell when you really, really want a cigarette, why did you ask me to be the judge in the first place? I say this is one of the times you're asking for a smoke just from habit."

Mike slouched against the door and sulked as the miles inched by. Finally, he spoke.

"You really ought to quit you know, like me. I just decided one day last week to stop, and I'm glad I did. Cigarettes are dangerous to your health and they cost too much. At last I can really taste food and my breath doesn't smell like a dead skunk. I can breathe a lot better too. All it takes is a little will power and common sense."

Mike Dineen is a great guy and a true friend. I decided not to kill him. After all, who else would hop a bus and travel five hundred miles to help me haul a load of horses from New Jersey to Georgia? He was then working at a station in Pittsburgh. He may have weird thought patterns, but what veteran Disc Jockey is normal? There was no radio in the beat-up old truck, so what's wrong with his playing that static-spewing boondocks blaster radio roughly the size of my college rental house that he constantly fiddles with? So it didn't work out for him to share the driving because he insists on putting along at thirty-five miles an hour on I-95 with monstrous semi trucks blowing by us on both sides. So what?

I kept repeating those thoughts to myself. It's a two-thousand mile round trip and there were two more loads to haul, and besides, his family knows where he went and justifiable or not, I would be the number one suspect when his body was identified.

About five minutes later, he requested another cigarette and again I refused to give him one, reminding him to exercise that iron will. He struck like a cobra. His hand shot out and grabbed the shirt pocket where the deadly coffin nails were located, ripping the material as he clutched desperately at the crumpled pack.

Caught by surprise, I lurched backward and struck at his hand, nearly losing control of the awkward vehicle. We swerved and wobbled from lane to lane on the interstate. I could hear the six horses in the rear bouncing off the walls. Finally, trembling and shaken I regained control of the truck as Dineen calmly inhaled another drag from one of the few remaining cigarettes.

"How many were you smoking before you.quit," I asked through gritted teeth.

"Almost two packs a day."

"According to my calculations, based on your bumming rate of one every fifteen minutes, and assuming you don't smoke in your sleep, you are now smoking at the rate of three and a half packs a day. When we stop for gas, I'm going to buy you a pack so you'll quit driving me nuts and trying to wreck us."

"Oh sure," he yelled. "Try to get me hooked again. You're a real pal."

The move back to the Peach State wasn't exactly peachy as the old truck broke down on the third trip and left the family and two dogs stranded in Maryland for nearly a week. The farm turned out to be a long-abandoned, unbelievably primitive dump that we spent the next few months making livable. It was also just outside Bowman near the South Carolina state line, exactly one hundred miles from the WQXI parking lot. We were trapped there for a year and a half before moving closer to Atlanta.

Clay Sledge put in a word for me to Program Director Bill Sherard and I began filling in as the temporary all night DJ and running the board for Atlanta Falcons broadcasts. The permanent position was earmarked for a minority person partly because an African American man that I had hired with the permission of the three Bs had held the position.

Since 1970, George Strait had been holding down the midnight to 6 A M shift before leaving for a TV job in Philadelphia, and I don't mean the Country singer. George had called me in New Jersey for my opinion on whether or not he should take the television offer and I advised him to go for it. He was soon appearing on the ABC TV network and then moved to CBS TV where he was their medical reporter for several years. He was a highly educated young man who had been wasting his abilities as an all-night DJ. When he applied for the job at Quixie he was a cab driver with a master's degree.

When I finished an all-night shift I liked to hang around at least an hour or two for the Gary McKee show partly because I was dreading the 100 mile drive home but mostly because it was so much fun. McKee was a flat out great Disc Jockey, blessed with a voice that reached out and grabbed a listener's attention. He always sounded as if he was having a terrific time on the air, laughing, cracking jokes and interacting with callers and staff members. I was soon joining the party, contributing lines and character voices on the show.

Bill Sherard demanded a more music, less talk, tight format for the rest of the day parts but wisely encouraged a lot of humor and information on the morning show. He seemed to appreciate my contributions and before long I was added to the cast, joining newsman Dan Gray and Bob Carr who played a character called Willis the Guard. Bob had been an announcer on the old WKXI FM station which played instrumental music and featured financial news before Sherard was designated to turn it into WQXI FM an album oriented rock music station. Kent Burkhart and George Burns were no longer involved since Pacific and Southern had sold their stations to Jefferson Pilot Insurance.

Bob Carr had been dropping in on the McKee show doing comedy bits in a character voice reminiscent of Gomer Pyle. His character was supposedly the station's security guard, an easy-going redneck from Cumming, Georgia. Willis the Guard became quite popular with the audience and when the FM station changed formats and the McKee show was simulcast on both AM and FM, Bob Carr was made a permanent member of the McKee morning show. Bob and I spent a lot of time together dreaming up bits and jokes. We became close friends and since Gary McKee was not eager to accept outside appearances, Bob and I teamed up many times to fill the requests for nightclub stand-up and MC duties. I wrote most of the material as I like to be prepared while laid back Willis preferred to have a few beers and wing it.

Dan Gray left for a news job in St. Louis and David Collin was hired as News Director. He became part of the morning team as a straight man for Mckee. Dave was a serious, hard-nosed news chaser who morphed into a human laugh track when interacting with Gary McKee. Since there was no provision for a comedy writer in the programming budget, my less than enormous salary came out of the news budget. Dave sometimes attempted to keep me on duty after the morning show, assigning me to cover speeches and news conferences at City Hall or the State Capitol or to roam around shopping centers to solicit opinions on current events from surly strangers. With a hundred mile drive back to my barely inhabitable farm home I was not interested in hanging around town and playing cub reporter. I didn't mind reading the news, I just hated gathering it.

The only times I enjoyed being in the newsroom were when I was writing jokes or chatting with Sachi Koto, a beautiful young lady of Japanese heritage. The first time I worked with her I was filling a weekend DJ slot and she was making her debut on the air. I complimented her on the smooth news delivery and we struck up a friendship. She was always interested in hearing about my horses and my family. My young children Brian and Susan loved Sachi and she invited them to spend a few weekends at her home.

Sachi was a dedicated worker with a beautiful voice and had previously been a successful model. As I feared, she was too pretty and talented for radio and was lured away by WAGA TV to become an on-camera reporter. She and her husband moved to Japan for several years where she continued to work in television and radio. After returning to America she joined CNN as a news anchor for the next sixteen years before starting her own communications and public relations firm specializing in Asian clients.

Another multi-talented lady to join the news department was Yetta Levitt who quickly became a big asset to the Gary McKee show. Yetta was an actress who could laugh on cue at even the weakest of jokes as well as ad-lib brilliantly. Her feminist-leaning intellect was a fine counter balance to good ole boy McKee and the country hick Willis character. She also went into TV, but managed to hold down her news anchor position on the Gary McKee show along with a noontime show on WXIA TV Channel Eleven. As if that weren't enough, she also frequently acted in plays at night.

Bill Sherard had moved on to another job in Mobile, Alabama and Scott Shannon was hired as the new Program Director. Scott encouraged the team approach to the morning show which was probably the first in AC radio. Its success, like any success in radio was soon copied almost everywhere and it is now a rarity to hear a lone Disc Jockey attempting to carry a morning show. Gary McKee was a great DJ with the sense to share the microphone and use the talents of other team members. Not that no ego conflicts arose, but the show set the standard for morning entertainment and the personalities remain lifetime friends.

Scott Shannon hired some strong personalities to fill the day parts, including Larry "Night Train Lane" Zachery, J. J. Jackson, Rhett Walker and Coyote McCloud. Shannon held down the afternoon drive time shift. He also brought an assistant with him from the Nashville station he had programmed previously to taking the job at WQXI. Shannon recognized potential in a young guy fresh out of college by the name of Don Benson. He eventually ended up as the President of the entire radio division.

The station lost an excellent DJ and Music Director when "Doctor" John Leader resigned to accept a job in Los Angeles with Radio and Records, the leading industry publication. Fortunately, radio still had many so-called "Doctors."

Red Necks, White Socks and Blue Ribbon Beer

Driving a hundred miles to work in the wee hours, I listened to radio. Though they have all but disappeared from the AM dial, at that time there were several all-night shows catering to truck drivers on 50,000 watt stations. We were experiencing the CB radio craze which originated with long haul truckers and spread to the general motoring public. Millions of people were driving around, speaking in code with a hillbilly twang, ten-four-ing and good buddy-ing like a bunch of moonshiners trying to outfox the Smokies with their mobile radios. I was getting all the microphone usage I wanted so I never got into the CB craze. It did give me an idea though.

I suggested that Willis should record a very simple, repetitive truck driving song and he liked the idea. He came up with a clever ditty about shifting gears and drinking beer and driving his truck all over the world. He recorded it with some instrumental music and gave it to McKee to play on the show. It became a hit on the request line and before long a man called with an offer. Tom Wright owned a recording studio and he wanted to record not only the song which Willis titled, Drive My Truck, he wanted to do an entire album.

Willis, McKee and I went to work writing redneck songs. Willis penned a surprisingly good narration effort called PBRs and Peanuts, about a lonely guy longing for a lost love while seated in a bar drinking Pabst Blue Ribbon beer and snacking on peanuts. Trust me, the song sounds better than the description. McKee knocked out several clever and humorous numbers. I contributed two songs, one being the popular Buford Triangle, a takeoff on the Bermuda Triangle legend of mysterious disappearances. I wrote a few more, but with all three of us grinding out novelty songs we had more than needed for an album.

Every day for a few weeks when the show ended we headed for the recording studio where along with Tom Wright's employed musicians, whom McKee dubbed The Crimson Cowboys, Willis sang and recited our strange lyrics.

News Director Dave Collin was recruited to act as our album cover photographer and Willis, McKee and I posed in hats and jeans in front of a rustic building. I had a primitive darkroom operation at home where I developed the black and white shots. The finished album looked just about right for the countrified, truck driving novelty songs.

The album's songs got tons of requests and several thousand copies were sold in the metro area but in reality it was just another morning show bit. Some conflicts arose when Willis started to take his singing career too seriously and McKee accused him of trying to take all the credit for the album. Willis Caswell and The Crimson Cowboys made a handful of local appearances to less than wild applause and after a few weeks the album became an afterthought with a song played only occasionally. There is a time to get off any bit. The whole CB/ trucker craze was itself short lived, or should I say, "over."

Won't Be Fooled Again

The ratings were soaring on the AM station and even on WQXI FM from 6 to 10 AM during the McKee Morning Show, but the FM numbers were far behind AM the rest of the day. The Rock of Georgia as Bill Sherard had dubbed the FM switch from business news and instrumental music had achieved only minor success.

One of the FM Jocks was Steve Clark, a guy I had worked with at WCPO and WWDJ. Sherard was unhappy with his nonchalant performance and called him into his office. When asked why he had accepted the job in Atlanta, Clark replied, "For the chicks on the phone," and was fired. No points for honesty.

A common irritant for radio people is to be approached by a listener who accuses them of not looking like they sound. A more ridiculous statement would be difficult to find outside of an acid rock album, and I always enjoyed pointing out that looks do not make noise. Of course, what they were trying to convey was that they had drawn a different mental image of the radio person. This can work both ways as someone on the phone may project an image quite different from his or her actual appearance.

Gary McKee told of a young lady with a beautiful voice who was a regular caller to his show. He liked to put her on the air once in a while and since it was in his bachelor days he got around to asking her for a luncheon date. They agreed to meet at Morrison's Cafeteria next door to the station. The young lady's father drove her to the meeting place and opened the car door for her. McKee was quite surprised to see that the girl with the lovely voice was a blind dwarf.

Trouble began to brew when a few employees decided that Scott Shannon was mistreating and over-working the staff. They started a movement to unionize the stations, calling in AFTRA, the American Federation of Television and Radio Artists, for a vote. The big honchos based in Charlotte, North Carolina were quite upset at the thought of dealing with a union and threatened that heads would roll should the vote be in favor of AFTRA. GM Jerry Blum promised the employees that steps would be taken to improve morale and that the company would give them everything the union could provide without paying dues. The vote to unionize failed and soon Shannon was fired.

The next person to settle into the Program Director's hot seat was Jack Fitzgerald. He brought along a crew of highly creative but somewhat strange writers, air personalities and assistants. Fitzgerald took over the midday shift on AM but most of the staff was retained. He and his cohorts conjured up what they thought would be a great way to kick off the Jack Fitzgerald era in Atlanta radio, the end of WQXI.

For weeks the station ran recorded promos and aired hundreds of announcements that as of three PM on a certain day, the hit music and all that Quixie had ever been would come to an end forever. Hundreds of T shirts imprinted with the message were given away. They were even sent to all the ad agencies and radio stations in town. Someone blew his nose in one and sent it back. It was an omen.

The way to manipulate the Arbitron ratings, which all programmers try to do, is to get the audience to tune in at a certain time then write it in the listening diary provided to them by the ratings company. After decades, the Atlanta radio legend was going to end. Undoubtedly hundreds of thousands of past and present Quixie fans would be listening for the historical switch to some new format which would guarantee gigantic ratings. What could possibly go wrong, or have we dealt with that question before?

THIRTEEN

(Just Like) Starting Over

At three o clock on the fateful day, Jack Fitzgerald and his gang of merry prankster assembled in the main WQXI AM control room, overcome with gleeful impatience to play their masterpiece recording of the Quixie-ending announcement followed by a rousing version of There's No Business Like Show Business by Ethyl Merman, wild applause, laughter and the earth shattering news that nothing would change except instead of calling the station Quixie it would henceforth be referred to as, are you ready? The New Q X I! At three o clock plus about ten seconds something went wrong.

Just as Ethyl's grating rendition of the show biz anthem cranked up, the station began going off and on the air. For its one and only time the control room console shorted out. It went off for a few seconds, then came back on, then back off, then dead silence as Fitzgerald screamed for help from the station's engineers. I guess you can play practical jokes on the audience but don't mess with wires, transistors and circuit boards.They have no sense of humor.

Even without the ironic technical difficulties, the big switcheroo ploy was a complete disaster. It seems that neither listeners, sponsors nor other living things appreciate being played for fools. Believe it or not, one reason for the moronic decision to drop the nickname Quixie came from one of those shameless research organizations that charge broadcasters enormous amounts for trivial information and stupid advice. They informed management and programming that the decades-old title was offensive to women because it sounded too much like a quickie.

There is no doubt that some people constantly search for something they can label offensive and I have encountered several timid air personalities who seemed to live in fear of offending someone. Those weak individuals were quite insipid and boring on the air because all good entertainers are somewhat offensive to at least a small segment of the audience. One must offend them to win the praises of the rest of the crowd. I always tried my best to offend those hyper-sensitive few. Failing to do so would leave both them and the non-sensitive unfulfilled and disappointed.

The New QXI and WQXI FM were moved further north on world famous Peachtree Street to new and even flashier digs in Tower Place, a brand new, modernistic glass skyscraper. Jerry Blum supervised the interior décor, designing appropriate surroundings for a colorful and dynamic contemporary radio facility. The walls were painted a bright orange and purple accented with huge impressionistic portraits of rock music superstars. Visitors never failed to be impressed by the unexpected surroundings. Most loved it, others, not so much. Comedian Pat Paulson gazed at the floor to ceiling chrome tubing that complemented the orange and purple lobby and mumbled, "This place looks like the inside of an intestine."

There was no argument that the ratings were not pretty. Part of the audience felt that they had been lied to. Others took the station by its word and since it was leaving forever, they turned to our competition, WZGC FM, or as it was called, Z 93. When ratings go down revenue goes down. Account executives become irate, the GM is taking heat from the titled bosses at corporate headquarters and surly unrest prevails throughout the land. It is a stern reminder that show business is indeed a business.

There was only one way to win back those straying listeners. More clever promotions should do the trick. Fitzgerald came up with another one built around the ever-popular and current Civil War. He had the news department and Gary McKee announce that MARTA, the metro area public transportation organization, had made a fantastic discovery while digging an underground tunnel. The hoax featured a fake historian who claimed that the Confederacy had hidden hundreds of millions of dollars worth of gold as the Union Army advanced on Atlanta. In the destruction and confusion of war the vast treasure was lost and eventually forgotten. MARTA workers had stumbled upon it and a conspiracy to keep the gold for themselves was hatched by insiders in city government. The only point of the MARTA Gold promotion was to pull another knee-slapping, rib-tickling, ha ha you've been punked trick on the audience. For some strange reason the ratings went from bad to worse. Credibility? Whaz' at?

Pick Up the Pieces

The rumbles of discontent coming from the sales department grew to a roar and Clay Sledge started spreading the word that I should be put in charge of programming. Others thought Don Benson, Scott Shannon's former assistant was ready for the job. Eventually I was named Program Director of the AM station and Don was handed the FM reins. Jack Fitzgerald and his buddies exited stage left, humming, "There's no business like show business."

I moved into the big, fancy, glass-walled programming office fully aware that I was placing my neck on the chopping block. The second time around I even got to make some decisions. No Burkhart and Burns looking over my shoulder with Sylvia Clark as Music Director. Her, I soon missed.

From the first day of my move into the big office I was deluged with congratulatory phone calls, mostly from record promoters. I inherited another attractive secretary, Pam Bellamy, and she could actually type, take dictation and was good on the phones. As the term secretary was by then considered an outdated, chauvinistic insult, her title was Programming Assistant. She assured me she was thrilled that I was the new PD. The sales crew assured me they would give me their full support, the ladies in accounting, traffic, continuity, the news staff and most of the DJs assured me that they were elated to have me in charge of programming. Some of them were even sincere.

Music promoters made a living by befriending, schmoozing and flattering PDs and Music Directors in a never-ending quest to coerce, wheedle and cajole them into playing every stiff released. Pam stayed on the phone constantly with one promoter picking her brain for information about the new PD while another half-dozen or more waited on hold. They operate under the theory that everyone has a weakness, booze, babes, drugs, sports, payola, all those fun things we consider hobbies but can't afford.

Pam didn't know me very well either so she informed them that I was a family man who raised horses as a hobby. Most of the slick Hollywood and New Yorker types found it a little difficult to buddy up by faking interest in equine agriculture. There were local promoters, regional promoters, national promoters and most aggressive of all, independent promoters. The poor local guys had more bosses than I did during my first go round as Program Director.

When I had very little to do with music ads, I neither knew nor cared how the radio/records system worked. A record added on a major station such as WQXI was worth six points in the leading trade publications and determined the fate of most releases. A six point add caused the song to rise on the national hit list, and if it made a big jump it rose "with a bullet," signaling a hit.

Superstar artists didn't need much help from radio as their songs nearly always sold well. Adding a record was a big boost, dropping one off the playlist could kill it. Radio Music Directors collected sales results from selected stores each week to track the rise or fall of current recordings. Generally, three or four new songs made the station's list each week and an equal number fell off. Record reps whose careers depended on their ability to obtain air play almost always utilized two approaches, let's have dinner or much more often, let's go get drunk.

Observing the many other Programmers who had come and gone, some of whom tended to believe they really were as great as the people with agendas told them they were, only to be discarded like yesterday's trash. I kept reminding myself that Program Directors were hired to be fired, just a nice buffer between the ratings and upper management. A hit song in hot rotation at the time snapped me back to reality whenever I started to think perhaps all these people were right and I really was something special. Oh, there's that Eagles song again.

It reminds me to remember who I am and that everybody loves a new kid only until somebody newer comes along.

The coveted Music Director position was foisted off on mid-day Jock Rhett Butler. Some people crave aggravation. He was much more into music than I was and didn't mind a few cocktails with the promoters. The music people correctly assumed that I would retain the final decisions on music adds and though Rhett filtered many of their frantic hypes they still called and dropped by my office. I tried to be as accommodating as I could while protecting the sound and integrity of the station because I realized that they were doing their jobs and we needed them as they needed us.

Rhett was a good DJ and a good Music Director before resigning to become a music promoter. Frying pan, meet fire. If there was any field less secure than radio it was music promotion. I hired Mitch Braswell who had been a DJ on the FM station under Bill Sherard as Rhett's replacement.

We had a fine staff of personalities beginning with the Gary McKee Morning Show, then Rhett, and J. J. Jackson, whom I had convinced Jerry Blum we should rehire. He had taken a job in Detroit and wanted to return to Quixie. I knew the feeling after being in the North homesick for Atlanta every day. Night Train Lane still held down the midnight hours and Jerry gave me a little surprise when he announced that he had hired Chase and Woodside to fill the afternoon traffic slot.

Barry Chase had left Quixie during the Sherard regime and teamed up with former WQXI newsman Scott Woodside at Z 93. They had a highly rated morning show for a few years and Jerry thought they could be successful on our station. They achieved good ratings for a while but FM competition eroded those numbers before long.

FM radio had finally boomed in Atlanta, especially on our sister station, WQXI FM which Don Benson had named 94Q. Across town PD John Young had Z93 competing and a hard rock station, WKLS FM aka 96Rock was the choice for teens trying to appear hip. Quixie's biggest competition was right down the hall, second door on the right.

WQXI AM and WQXI FM were targeting the same demographic audience. The McKee show was simulcast on both stations and it was like two lovers spending a great morning together, and then going their separate ways, cheating, manipulating and striving mightily to outfox one another. Since I brought it up, there was also an FM Oldies station WFOX to contend with. One more time I found myself struggling with a puny, underpowered AM signal. The late 70s was not a good time for anyone trying to run a music format on AM radio.

August 16, 1977 I was surprised to receive a phone call from Sachi Koto. She was on duty at Channel 5, and she had not called to chat. She was trying to confirm a shocking rumor that Elvis Presley had died suddenly. I put her on hold and dialed RCA promotion President Eddie Mascola in Nashville. False rumors of celebrity deaths are fairly common and I presumed that this would be another one. Mascola unhesitatingly informed me that it was true. Elvis had died that morning in Memphis. I gave Sachi the confirmation and her TV station and our radio station scooped the world with the breaking news.

Chase and Woodside were on the air and I informed them of Elvis' demise. I began typing up memorial lines to the King of rock and roll and turned the afternoon team loose to do a tribute show. They grabbed every Elvis album in the music library and began to ad lib around the songs. They were at their very best that day. No one could have given them a better scripted program than the one they presented with only a few lines I had written and the songs they selected. They say people of that generation will always remember where they were when they heard of the deaths of JFK and Elvis. They are certainly right.

Shut Up and Dance

In December of '77 a movie starring John Travolta had a huge influence on both radio and pop music. Saturday Night Fever launched the Disco era as discotheques sprang up everywhere. Former singles bars morphed into singles bars with mirrored, revolving globes, strobe lights, smoke machines, enormous sound systems and thumping dance music.

The men hung out clad in off-white suits and platform shoes trying to look like Travolta's movie character, Tony Manero. Fuzzy Afro hairdos, and wide-collared paisley shirts unbuttoned to the navel exposing gold chains were all the rage. I don't recall such strange disco fashions for women. For once it was the men who fell for the comical fashion trends. Suddenly it seemed the entire male population had started dressing like record promoters.

A national record rep from California, who sported all of the aforementioned except the platforms, substituting ballerina slippers without socks, recommended that I follow the hip trends. Old guys who dress like rebellious teens never realize how ridiculous they look. My wife and three teenage kids would have been quick to remind me by laughing themselves sick if I had ever tried to look hip.

The Bee Gees shot to super stardom via the Saturday Night Fever soundtrack. The Bee Gees I sort of liked, but soon we were inundated with disco records by the hundreds, even re-mixes of old songs including an album by Elvis. Some Country artists such as Bill Anderson had disco hits. Club DJs became well-paid stars in some of the larger venues and radio jocks were in high demand for outside work. Chase and Woodside went into business with their own equipment they called The Portable Peach. Record spinners in discos were important influences in music sales and were being courted by record reps.

It was hard to avoid being hired to host disco dances. I disliked most of them because of the diverse musical tastes of the party-goers. When the alcohol is flowing freely, the poor DJ is the target of scorn with practically every record he plays. The country crowd demands more Country music, the old fogies send an underling to demand Glen Miller and all big band sounds, the teens threaten to destroy the sound system unless they get all hard rock, heavy metal stuff and half of the people want all slow records while the other half goes into a rage unless the poor DJ plays all up-tempo noise. It is standard practice for someone in the crowd to demand access to the microphone to do a drunken speech or attempt to organize a boring game. Through it all, I managed to keep focusing on the money.

On the air it was dance, dance, dance to such masterpieces as a remake of a Beethoven symphony to Disco Duck by Rick Dees and His Gang of Idiots. Even pre-schoolers could share in disco mania.They committed sacrilege by issuing a Beatles disco medley. Radio jocks were attempting to mix one bumping booty tune with the next in a smooth segue just like the club DJs practiced to keep the dancers on the floor. Ballads and good old fashioned rock music found it hard to crack the charts and receive airplay. I knew disco was destined to be a passing fad. I just didn't think the next music craze would be even worse.

FOURTEEN

The Race Is On

The Kidney Foundation approached me as Program Director asking for assistance in raising awareness of kidney disease and fund raising. Since the Ramblin' Raft Race, aka Chattahoochee River Festival was the biggest and best participatory radio promotion ever, I conjured up visions of a similar event on land.

Larry Patrick was approached and recruited to assist in organizing the event. He suggested we simply call it The Great Race, borrowing the title from a movie. My plan was to allow vehicles and contraptions in different categories, anything without a motor, to race about four miles from Buckhead to the Atlanta Fulton County Stadium. Recalling all the strange and fantastic floating conveyances that showed up for the raft races, I expected even wilder spectacles designed for land usage. The event would be a great party/parade with broad appeal for spectators. Then the Kidney Foundation officials became involved.

Charities can be quite helpful in supplying manpower for promotions, but I soon learned that those who saw themselves as important executives couldn't resist giving orders and making changes. I was donating tens of thousands of dollars worth of air time and the promotional expertise of myself and Larry Patrick.

We had decided that roller skates, bicycles, skateboards, pushed or pulled wagons, rick shahs, beds, bathtubs or anything that moves by human power alone could compete. We encouraged costumes and offered prizes for the most outlandish. It was a fine concept until I learned after the fact that a boss at the Kidney Foundation had gotten antsy and decided we were not receiving enough entries. Patrick and I realized that the race would have to become an annual event and build up year to year exactly as the raft races had done.

Without consulting me someone from the foundation had approached a well-known runner to involve The Atlanta Track Club and turn the whole thing into just one more rather boring foot race. Soon I started receiving calls from people at the charity's office complaining about how the DJs were wording the promos and trying to tell me how to run the station. Naturally I was furious and let fly with a few expletives. The offended amateur programmer immediately called GM Jerry Blum and reported me but he didn't seem to care once I explained the situation.

The Great Race went off as scheduled with a lot of runners and perhaps a total of a hundred or so miscellaneous entries, far less than I had anticipated before the event became branded as just another dull race with not much to look at other than sweaty, skinny runners. The race wasn't so great after all and it was the only one we attempted.

Static and Interference
(From the sales department)

Radio programmers fight a constant battle with sales departments that will destroy a station with their money grubbing demands for more and more commercial time, trashy contests and boring remotes. Live, on-site broadcasts are easiest to sell, but few things sound worse than a DJ in a used car lot trying to ad lib about six live spots an hour, stumbling and groping for one more way to say the same old "Come join us and get the deal of a lifetime." Account execs are usually nonchalant about supplying copy or even basic information. I did a lot of remotes as a DJ and most were flops. Unless you are giving away something worth coming out for it gets quite lonely. Those who arrive to snare a free hotdog or record album do not come to buy high ticket items. For instance something as expensive as a can of motor oil or a soft drink. The sales rep is rarely on hand, leaving the DJ to catch the complaints and scornful looks from the proprietor.

Sales people always seem to have a bunch of crummy products they want to give away on the air. This is the result of promising a client a promotion with a gazillion free plugs if he will buy a schedule of spots. When Craig Ashwood of 94Q was a PD in Washington D.C., a salesperson wanted him to air a promotion for a building supply company, "Call in and win a brick."

A monkey hear, monkey do gimmick called Commercial Free Mondays swept through copycat radio but I declined to slap it on the AM station since it only draws attention to commercials and implies the station is listenable one day a week and destroys consistence in sound, one of the main strengths of music radio. Pseudo programming expert Sales Manager, Bill Phippin thought it was such a terrific idea he pulled an end run and told the people in the traffic department to simply not schedule any spots on Monday. So we crammed them in on top of the regular spot load on Tuesday.

Sales-oriented management types will try any method but common sense. Having tried the sales route beginning with magazines at the age of six and learning that I couldn't sell ham sandwiches in a famine, I admire and respect sales people and some are lifelong friends. I lost nearly all my customers when

The Saturday Evening Post raised the cover price from a dime to fifteen cents.

Pam Bellamy, Programming Assistant had a dream of living and working in fabulous Los Angeles. I can think of very few things that sound less appealing, but eventually a record company offered her a job and she resigned to head west. It was time to start interviewing applicants for the vacant position.

One young lady struggled to fill out an application and when I interviewed her she said she would like to start the following Monday. She also wanted her one-week paid vacation to begin Monday and assured me that she would then be ready for duty after her much deserved break. She didn't get the job.

We hired Joan Schwartz, an intelligent and efficient worker who was eager to advance in the business, so much so that whenever I was out of town on a business trip she allegedly took the opportunity to meet with the GM, tell him how bad I was as a Program Director and pitch for my job. Back when we called them secretaries they were supposed to be loyal to their bosses. A few months answering phones hardly qualifies one to program a major radio station though most people think they could handle the job just by playing their favorite records.

Among several drawbacks to the PD position is baby-sitting Disc Jockeys, notoriously immature whiners in real life after being forced to fake perennial happiness on the air. The normal routine was, finish the show, and make a bee-line to Corry's office to ask for a big raise, more time off, a better shift, an on-air assistant, a secretary, a company car and a personal key to the prize closet. Dealing with talented people is always a challenge and all of our Jocks were asked for much more than the liner-reading, computer operators of today. You might be a Disc Jockey running no-talk, ten record sweeps but you are in no way a personality.

Weekend DJ Randy Blake and a buddy who was a newsman at Country station WPLO were having a few drinks one night in downtown Atlanta. Randy began to pine for an old girlfriend who lived about fifty miles away in Conyers. The guys had no car available so they acted like drunken radio guys and stole a city bus. Now that's personality.

A trusting driver had left the bus idling outside a hotel and the fellows assuming he didn't want it anymore, jumped in and headed East on I-20. Whatever they had been drinking worked wonders.

Arriving at work the next day at my usual, rush hour traffic avoiding 9:30, I was deluged with demands that I check the morning edition of the Atlanta Constitution, the radio-despising newspaper. Adorning the front page was a photo of a MARTA bus, half a page wide with huge headlines screaming, WQXI Disc Jockeys Steal Bus. The stop-the- presses, special edition story detailed how the dangerous culprits had been halted and arrested and how through great police work the bus was recovered.

Jerry Blum and I met to discuss the crime and to determine the employment status of Mr. Blake. Jerry was surprisingly calm and I was trying not to laugh aloud over the incident. We agreed that the newspaper coverage and undoubtedly the forthcoming breaking news bulletins on TV were fine publicity for the station considering the throng of uncouth hooligans that made up our target audience. I informed a somewhat sheepish Randy Blake that he would not be fired if he promised to steal no more buses.

Being no judge of newsworthiness, I am curious as to why the purloined bus was a much bigger story to local media than the van driver capers. I suspect it slipped past them unnoticed. We had a station van with call letters painted all over it that we used to haul portable sound systems to remote broadcasts and disco parties. Our part time drivers would set up the equipment at the location and were supposed to hang around to assist the DJ. One mild-mannered fellow would always come up with an excuse to leave for awhile, to buy cigarettes, or to get a sandwich to go. He was actually getting some cash to go, but not from an ATM. He was pulling holdups at convenience stores.

"Officer Wiggins, Ma'am. Do you have a description of the vehicle he was driving?"

"Yes officer, it was a silver-gray van with orange and purple stripes, and bright red, yellow and blue letters on both sides that said WQXI and 94Q."

"Hmm, so you didn't get the number on the license plate?"

Through more great police work the perp was tracked down and apprehended. That guy we fired, and there was barely a mention by our local news gatherers. On the police blotter it was just a line in the daily convenience store holdup column.

Our other van drivers were much better. All I caught them doing was taking prizes from the closet and instead of loading the good stuff into the van to take to a remote, they were stashing them in a dumpster to be retrieved later.

It was never boring. I loved going to work every day and actually disliked weekends and holidays. It was a wonderful time in a fantastic facility full of interesting people. To have fun on the air I did the 6 to 10 A. M. Saturday morning show simulcast on both AM and FM and filled in frequently for McKee when he was on one of his many vacations. He had a European type contract where they take more time off than a school teacher.

FM radio was getting more popular all the time and 94Q led by Don Benson was achieving all time high ratings. If AM radio was to survive, changes had to be made. The ratings were up significantly from the New QXI crash, but the big brains at corporate headquarters in Charlotte claimed our measly signal should be capturing ratings similar to those of their 50,000 watt clear channel station in Charlotte, WBT. I suppose this ludicrous conclusion was the result of insurance company executives being put in charge of broadcast facilities.

Catching grief for doubling the ratings wasn't bad enough. Don Benson and I flew to the headquarters of Arbitron, the company that took ratings by mailing diaries to selected residents. They were to make notes on their daily listening habits and mail them back to Arbitron. We were allowed to visit their offices to review the results. I thought it an expensive waste of time but one must play the game so off into the wild blue yonder we went to Columbia, Maryland in early March.

Don and I were wandering around the Washington D.C. area looking for a good place to have an expense account dinner. I talked him into stopping at a joint owned by a former major league baseball player because I've always been a fan. The food was somewhere between mediocre and bad. I would say it hit about 300. We rented a room and for some dumb reason, settled for one room with two beds. Whenever I dozed off, Benson yelled at me to stop snoring. Long night, short naps.

The next day we checked in early at Arbitron headquarters. They had more security than Fort Knox to protect those precious diaries. We had to pass the ID checkpoint, were issued passes to wear around our necks at all times and were escorted down long halls to a tiny cubicle containing a tray of hastily scrawled alleged diaries. The nervous guy keeping a close eye on us was a dead ringer for Floyd the Barber on the old Andy Griffith Show and Benson couldn't keep from snickering whenever he talked and gestured.

The diaries were a mess of confusion with some respondents writing down TV shows rather than radio programs. No problem for Arbitron. If an addled soul wrote down Gomer Pyle on WSB TV, they credited it to WSB radio. My luck, the old WQXI TV station had been changed to WXIA so I was not the beneficiary of TV morphed into radio shows.

Another well known, but conveniently ignored problem with measuring listenership by the diary method is the phony culture syndrome wherein people tend to lie about what they listen to by upgrading rotgut Country or Acid Rock to classical music or news on Public Radio. Nevertheless, the Arbitron diary method was accepted by the multi-billion dollar industry as gospel.

We had been aware that some snow might fall during the day, and sure enough, about 9:30 it looked like a holly jolly Christmas on the other side of Arbitron's bulletproof windows. Quickly deciding that our careful scrutiny of the diaries was complete we checked out with Floyd and made our way through the blizzard to the airport, turned in the rental car and boarded the flight for Atlanta.

Benson got the window seat, I had to settle for the middle seat and a huge, bearded man squeezed into the aisle seat. I was somewhat cramped but so what? We would be in Atlanta, free from the snow and cold in less than two hours. However, there was a long line of planes waiting for clearance to take off. The Flight Attendants attempted to assuage the impatient passengers by serving booze. My big seatmate kept ordering vodka and tonic would then reach inside the enormous coat he was wearing, dig out a bottle of whiskey and pour a double shot into the mix.

We sat there in stifling heat for hours as the snow continued to fall. The big galoot passed out and kept falling over onto me and I kept shoving him back over as Benson chortled at the buffoonery. After one of the longest days of my life we finally took off only to be greeted by heavy fog in Atlanta delaying our landing. We finally touched down at the end of a runway where we had to be bused to the terminal, arriving just before midnight. We had been on that boozy, stifling hot plane since around 10:30 A.M. You do the math. I'm still too disgusted to think about it.

Another trip to D.C. came about through an invitation to a White House meeting. Major market Programmers were summoned for an unrevealed reason and the gathering was not to be mentioned on air. The Secret Service ran a security check on me and I passed in spite of some of the Jimmy Carter jokes I had written. A hundred or so radio people met in the White House annex, so I sort of visited the White House, which was actually down a long hall. National Security had not been breached and finally the reason for flying in people from all reaches of America was revealed.

Paul Drew, a successful programmer and former WQXI DJ was hosting a meeting to ask for suggestions on how radio could keep teens from using illegal drugs. Paul is the same man who promoted Hands Across America, an ambitious project in which people were to hold hands in a human chain stretching from the Atlantic to the Pacific. Why? I guess because there was nothing good on TV that weekend.

When the reason for the meeting was announced, mumbling and rumbling from disappointed participants was noticed. Everyone had anticipated much more than an hour of, "We could run more public service announcements. We could host drug free parties. We could give away T shirts with anti-drug messages to the tenth caller," and those were the best ideas.

Hey You, Get Off'a Mc Cloud!

The AM ratings slipped a bit in the winter book and the pressure built. I had to make serious changes leading into the most important rating period of the year in April and May. That is the one which ad agencies rely on to determine time buys.

Scott Woodside was fired, breaking up the talky afternoon team. Evening Jock Coyote McCloud was let go as his high energy, teen-oriented approach was outdated and most of the teens lived in outlying suburbs which the station couldn't even reach. I replaced him on the 6 to10 PM shift with Brenda Miller, a smooth-voiced African American woman from our news department. Second-guessing programming specialists in sales reacted as if I had dynamited the transmitter. A female DJ? Horrors!

There had been several women doing fine work in the news department for many years but no one had worked up the courage to try a lady DJ. Since our hideous 1,000 watt directional nighttime signal only covered the urban area, I thought Brenda might attract a sizable following. She did, but after a few months she resigned because she did not like working nights.

The playlist was pared to only the hottest records during the month-long ratings period and the top five were played every hour and a half in morning and afternoon drive times. That was another terrible move according to sales department expertise. Shortly after the ratings period ended and before the results were available, I was replaced as AM Program Director by Don Benson.

Instead of being summarily canned as other scapegoat PD's had always been, I was offered the Promotion Director job which I accepted. A huge load had been lifted off my back, and I returned to doing what I do best, creating humorous promotions and submitting bits for the Gary McKee Morning Show. It was somewhat satisfying when the ratings results arrived showing the AM station had a big gain in listeners, especially the Brenda Miller Show. However in the interest of job security. I had learned not to snicker too loudly.

FIFTEEN

You Don't Have To Be a Weatherman
To See Which Way the Wind Blows

Many of my friends and supporters thought that I accepted the move downward on the company chain of command quite calmly. Truth be told, I could see that music formats on major market AM radio were doomed, not just on low-powered, energy-saving peanut cookers, but even the big boys with 50,000 watts were not going to compete with FM.

I never felt comfortable in that big orange and chrome office with nothing but glass separating me from the outside world. The geniuses who designed Tower Place either deliberately or stupidly neglected to install light switches and the glaring fluorescent lighting gave anyone on the outside that might be patronizing the nearby movie complex, restaurants and bars a creepy, prying view of the innards.

Many of my record promoting pals who had vowed to be lifetime friends deserted me like I had an infectious case of Nerdism. One shuck and jive huckster of stiffs phoned and launched into his false flattery, inviting me and my wife to dinner. I interrupted to inform him that I was no longer a PD and that Don Benson was now programming both stations. His next words, and the last words he ever spoke to me were, "Can you connect me to his office?"

Independent promoter Jimmy Davenport, whom we all called Otis or The Old Bear and I remained good friends and Don Miller who had made plans to treat Dixie and I to a dinner on our wedding anniversary insisted that the date was still on. He sent a Rolls Royce limousine to chauffeur us to and from the restaurant. Nice wheels for a lowly Promotion Director who had no influence with music.

Shortly after I escaped from the PD chair, the points for music adds were switched from WQXI AM over to 94Q making it the station reporting to the trade publications. Suddenly no one in the business cared about chart action on the AM station. Fleetwood Gruver who had been recording commercials and promos in the production studio was named Program Director of AM.

As Promotion Director I spent almost as much time fending off nonsensical pitches for on-air contests as I had received from record hypers. All of them had to be approved by Don Benson before they had a chance of making it onto the air anyway. Writing and dreaming up humorous promos was fun but paperwork, obtaining approvals and applying for permits, riding herd on our mischievous van drivers and trying to prevent wholesale theft of prizes by the sales department was stifling my creativity.

During that era Atlanta was one big cocktail party with a legal drinking age of 18. In cooperation with nightclubs or any business interested in attracting several thousand drunken guttersnipes the stations offered free beer to all comers. Budweiser and Miller were in a real battle for market share and they gladly furnished all the intoxicants our loyal listeners could guzzle. My job was to make sure the sound systems were set up and to hire enough police officers to maintain a semblance of civility. As unbelievable as it may seem, we never experienced a serious incident during or following one of our Happy Hour socials. The police performed their duties wonderfully and tended to overlook minor infractions partly because Benson had allowed a budget to pay them handsomely. I shudder to think what might have happened without their presence and I don't shudder easily.

Red Dawn

It was just another get together and idea exchange for new material to keep the Gary McKee Morning Show fresh and innovative, an informal meeting in Don Benson's office with McKee, Bob "Willis" Carr, Kelly McCoy and I trying to come up with a routine or character that hadn't already been done. Radio devours comedy material like a ravenous beast demanding fresh fodder every day. Having written for others, ad-libbed and performed literally thousands of bits in nearly twenty years of radio, the farthest thing from my mind was a life-changing experience.

We sat around joking, razzing one another as guys do, when at one point I started imitating a typical countrified caller complaining about the kind of music we play. Everyone laughed and Benson said, "Why don't you do something in that voice?" He suggested the character could do editorials. I agreed, with only a slight change. "Let's call them commentaries. That way he can take off on anything."

I already had a name picked out. Red Neckerson had been bouncing around in my head. I had at first envisioned him as a crusty old football coach who constantly yammered about the good, clean, all-American sport, inviting everyone to bring the whole family out to enjoy the game as we stomp, mutilate, crush, annihilate and destroy the enemy team. Sort of funny, but a one trick pony. I knew instantly that a commentator opened up a world of possibilities. The character could pontificate on unlimited topics concerning pop culture and common irritants.

Our meeting of brilliant minds occurred in mid February of 1979 and there happened to be some snow and ice on the roads. The first commentary I did as Red Neckerson was how Yahoos don't know how to drive in winter weather, but I certainly did because I had been up north, one time, all the way to Nashville. "Y'all need to wrap some old gunny sacks 'round yer tahrs and drive back'ards."

I typed up five commentaries in less than a half hour, taped them and McKee played one each day. By the end of the week Red was a radio star. It was a different time. Radio personalities were supposed to be ever happy, positive, friendly and warm. All of a sudden here was this angry old redneck just ranting and raving about everything and he was "accidentally" funny. I was an overnight success as Red Neckerson due to 20 years of preparation.

The Red character took off from the McKee Show launching pad. Bob Carr had the popular Willis the Guard bit down pat while on the air but he was adverse to staying in character when in public, going out of his way to inform everyone that he was actually a sophisticated suburbanite. I was determined to play the part of a good old boy redneck during public appearances to avoid disappointing our listeners, at least those who were a little slow at recognizing Gary Lee Corry's voice.

After a few weeks Red's reputation had spread to other markets. I was seated in my small, out of the way Promotion Director's office when I received a call from John Long, a friend of mine who was the Program Director of WHBQ, a major radio station in Memphis. His great morning Jock, Rick Dees was being transferred from WHBQ to their sister station in Los Angeles. John and former Quixie DJ Rusty Black were taking over the morning show and he wanted Red Neckerson's commentaries. I was flattered but quite reluctant to make a commitment. All I had heard from fellow radioites was the impossibility of syndicating anything, what a waste of time and talent it was, and why it would never succeed. Perhaps they never had anything worth syndicating. I also heard many sage comments warning how a redneck bit might be tolerated in Atlanta but the wrath of humanity would be unleashed upon any miscreant foolish enough to risk his crimson neck in any other locale.

When John Long told me that all he desired was for me to dub the tape I recorded for McKee, mail it to him and he would pay a hundred bucks a week, I was instantly in the syndication business.

Long had a nice budget from the salary they had been paying Dees, of Disco Duck fame. Some record promoter friends, Bill Lemons, Long John Silver, David Powell, Johnny Bee, and Jimmy Davenport began to hype Red to PDs in other markets and within a few months I was mailing tapes to fourteen stations around the Southeast.

In Atlanta, Red was hitting the clubs, emceeing, hosting, judging, making speeches and performing stand up. There were big newspaper articles and interviews as the press strove to reveal the real man behind the character. I learned that they tend to believe just about anything as long as it makes good copy. I told of attending college, majoring in broadcasting, taking many speech and announcing courses in an effort to lose my country accent. After years of remedial therapy I was able to work in major markets as both a newscaster and a Disc Jockey, but had never been rewarded with a top salary or national fame. Then I started talking like I did before I went to college and lo and behold, I started raking in the dough with the nationally syndicated redneck character. The moral of my rags to less ragged story was, remain true to yourself and do the best you can with what you have. Gets you right in the heart doesn't it?

In reality, I was born and raised in the Midwest and never had a noticeable accent, but the rest of it was pretty much true. Gary Lee Corry, aka Gary Russell was a good local DJ but so were a lot of other people. Red was becoming a star from coast to coast and beyond.

The Bill Moyes Media Research Company conducted a poll in Memphis and discovered that the market's most popular radio personality was some guy on WHBQ called Red Neckerson. Moyes, ever alert to hot trends and a chance to cash in, arranged for me to fly to Hartford, Connecticut where we met to discuss his company taking over the syndicate. We struck a deal and within a year Red was espousing wit and wisdom on over a hundred stations and the list kept growing and spreading like a computer virus.

WKRP
We Keep Replicating People

A hit TV series about a mythical radio station called WKRP debuted, produced by former Atlanta ad agency executive Hugh Wilson who had garnered plot lines and look-alike characters from research at WQXI. He interviewed several staff members including me when I was Program Director the first time. He took notes on nearly everything we mentioned and later used the information in episodes. He cast Gordon Jump, who looked a lot like GM Jerry Blum. Lori Anderson as receptionist Jennifer had all the attributes of Pam Bellamy with a lighter hair color. Sales guy Herb played by Frank Bonner, resembled our Sales Manager Clark Browne, though Clark denies it to this day. PD Andy Travis played by Gary Sandy roughly resembled Scott Shannon and Howard Hessman's role as Doctor Johnny Fever was either a tribute or an insult to Skinny Bobby Harper. I'm glad Hugh took note of all the "Doctors" turned DJ.

The most famous WKRP episode by far was the infamous Turkey Drop Thanksgiving tale wherein the station dropped live turkeys from a helicopter as station giveaways to lucky listeners. The inspiration came from a true story that Jerry Blum related to Hugh Wilson. Much has been written about the turkey drop, and most of it is wrong. It never occurred in Atlanta and no turkeys were thrown from the back of a truck as some claim. It happened in Dallas Texas as a KBOX promotion and the fat gobblers splattered in an unsightly manner when they hit the earth. It wasn't a matter of catching a free Thanksgiving turkey; it was scrape it up if you like carrion.

Despite ridiculous claims by other stations scattered across the country like drifting turkey feathers, WQXI was actually the first station to stage a fake turkey drop following the WKRP episode. In our theater of the mind, promotion, Red Neckerson was tossing turkeys off the roof of Tower Place to waiting contestants below. Production wizard Jack Cone produced whistling sound effects of a falling bird, followed by either loud cheers and applause or a loud, cartoonish boing as the correct caller attempted to "catch" it. Winners received certificates for turkeys from a supermarket and a red T shirt bearing station logos, a pair of hands and a drawing of a scared turkey along with the words, "I caught the turkey from WQXI." We thought it was a great contest. Research that came in months later said the audience hated it. These were the same people who laughed themselves silly at the TV version. You can't win 'em all. A few promotions are bound to be turkeys.

Who Says Breaking Up
Is Who Hard To Do?

Don Benson decided to break up the simulcast of the McKee show, relegating it to 94Q only. Fleetwood Gruver hired Jim Casey to keep the needle peaking on the AM morning show. Perhaps I should mention that the expression refers to the volume meter on the console which moves upward in reaction to sound input. If it's lying horizontally, it signals the catastrophic dead air syndrome. I liked to tell whoever followed me on the air to "just keep the needle peaking until a good Jock gets here."

To my surprise, the new dynamite AM lineup included me partnered with J. J. Jackson in afternoon drive. Not that I would miss sitting in my closet-sized office doing detail work, but a few words in advance would have been a little more professional. Sarah Rutledge, an experienced promotion person had been hired to take my place.

I soon agreed to make the switch to back on the air and even came up with a name for the show, J. J. and The Cowboy. It was the nickname some record promoters gave me even though I had no cows. City boys tend to think if one owns horses he must be a cowboy. It was a good name at that time because John Travolta of disco madness had struck again wreaking havoc on playlists.

The honky-tonk block buster movie Urban Cowboy starring Travolta and Deborah Winger was released and in a matter of days former disco queens and Tony Manero wannabees were sporting cowboy boots and ten gallon hats. Clubs were ripping out the disco equipment and installing mechanical bulls. Aping the movie action, guzzling beer from long neck bottles and fist fighting became the latest craze. I live in constant fear that John Travolta is somewhere plotting a new dance-oriented flick that will top his other two sociological tragedies.

J. J. and I were having a great time rolling with the flow, inventing comedy bits and regular characters while playing the hits that were suddenly interspersed with Waylon and Willie, Mickey Gilley and other Country singers not normally heard outside of an Appalachian moonshine festival.

Western wear store owners were getting richer than Jock Ewing and both Red and Cowboy were riding high.

Jim Davis, who played patriarch Jock Ewing on the number one TV show Dallas, made an appearance with J. J. and the Cowboy at the Omni in downtown Atlanta. Between sets we hung out with Mr. Davis and his wife in their suite. He was a congenial, down to earth man who treated us like old friends. My young daughter Susan accompanied me to the appearance and they were delighted to meet her. They told us how their own beloved daughter, an only child had been killed in an automobile accident. Jim related that he suffered periodically from excruciating cluster headaches, said to be many times worse than migraines and warned us that he would be screaming and bouncing off the walls if an episode occurred. Fortunately, that did not happen and we were saddened to hear not long after that bitter-sweet day that Jim Davis had died of a heart attack. I have met hundreds of celebrities over the years, some rude, some indifferent and some extremely nice people. I put Jim Davis in the nice category.

Among the cast of characters on the J.J. and the Cowboy show were The Complainers, a family dreamed up by J. J. that was always whining and complaining. The husband and father Brock, was the manager of a fast food restaurant called Liver King that served nothing but liver sandwiches with a side of spinach. They could not understand why business was slow. Comedian Joe Piscapo dropped by 94Q located just down the hall, and a few weeks later a regular skit began to appear on Saturday Night Live called The Whiners. Joe and his female partner, Robin Duke were getting laughs by constantly complaining about trivial matters. We never even got a thank you card.

Leaving On a Jet Plane

General Manager Jerry Blum had more nerve than any radio executive in America. He put out the word that all on-air personnel were to attend a mandatory meeting at Atlanta's Hartsfield International airport while part-timers kept the needles peaking. We were heading into an important ratings period and he had arranged for a world renowned motivational speaker to inspire us. The meeting had to be at the airport because the unnamed orator was only available between flights.

We arrived at the airport to be ushered into a private room where Jerry admitted that he was kidding us about a motivational speech and handed each of us an envelope with a plane ticket to New York City and $300 in cash for spending money. He had leased an entire wide-bodied 747 jet to chauffeur us to the Big Apple for a day of shopping, sight-seeing and dining just to get us in a good mood and do our best during the ratings month. We partied and joked with the flight attendants among the mostly empty seats in the huge plane. It was a great day with fine weather as we roamed the streets and stores of Manhattan and ended our day with a feast in a landmark Brooklyn steakhouse. I couldn't help but ponder how much the trip had cost the company and what the reaction of the sour-pussed bean counters at company headquarters would be in case the ratings were down. They weren't. The ratings showed a hefty gain and whatever the New York trip cost, it was another good investment as increased revenue poured in.

The Lights Went Out In Georgia

Don Benson accepted a big offer and left the company for a while and Jim Morrison, a 94Q DJ was appointed Program Director of the FM station. I recall his asking me for advice and my telling him the first thing he must learn to do is say "No." He thanked me for the advice many times. During his stint the stations were involved in a couple of gigantic mob scenes known as Light Up Atlanta. Proving that all they need is an excuse to party, hundreds of thousands of people gathered downtown just because office buildings agreed to leave the lights on and we showed up with the equipment to blast deafening dance music at them. I was perched on a trembling platform with a few other people, totally surrounded by the mass of dancing shouting humanity and it was a frightening experience that I do not care to experience again. One police officer kept mumbling that if trouble erupted they would be completely helpless. It was the raft race without the water doubled and crammed into a few city blocks. There were several kiosks selling beer and area bars did record business but no serious incidents occurred, once again proving my theory that The Lord watches over fools and drunks.

After the first two years of successful, energy wasting Light Up events, politics and resentments interceded as always whenever something is successful, and the city took over the promotion. The first year they were in charge, there were a couple of shootings, and the second year near-riots with broken store windows and looting. Lights out.

The final two raft races, known by then as Chattahoochee River Festivals were promoted exclusively on 94Q as WQXI AM became even less relevant to management. J.J. And the Cowboy ridiculed the snobbish FMers with Brock Complainer doing daily reports from his company's convention and rally, the Chattanooga Liver Festival.

Whatever it was called, the annual event on the river grew too big to survive and eventually suffered the same fate as Light Up. Politicians listening to the greatly exaggerated numbers of paid rafting entrants began asking where all that money was going and demanding a huge share for security and clean-up expenses. To further dampen enthusiasm for the promotion, one young man drowned the evening prior to the 1980 event. It was the first fatality after many years of heavy partying on and near sometimes dangerous waters, a near miracle as it is not rare for a drowning to occur on the river any given weekend.

We had decent ratings on the J. J. and the Cowboy show but Fleetwood kept telling J. J. to eliminate one bit after another to play more music. The problem was not our entertaining features. The problem was a music station trying in vain to compete with several FM stations. After a while it was two guys giving their names and cramming in as many old, burned-out ditties as possible. Believe it or not the ratings went down.

The team was split up and I was given the noon to three shift, then later moved to three to seven. The urban cowboy craze had ridden off into the sunset, none too soon and it was time to put the big hats, boots and western shirts in yard sales. Clubs and bars were trying desperately to sell their groin-crunching mechanical bulls. Many people thought the best thing the cowboy craze accomplished was to kill disco. I went back to the name I was given at birth with only the fake middle name, Lee. Scott Shannon had ordered me to add the Lee years before, to make my name different from Gary McKee's name, but his real middle name is Lee. He began calling himself Gary Lee McKee on the air for awhile so it pretty well defeated Shannon's purpose.

Helter Skelter

J. J. and production man and substitute DJ Harry Schuster filled the morning slot for a while, and then Harry and I were together in afternoons. The station had switched to an all oldies format as it fumbled for a market share. Someone finally deduced that both stations competing for the same audience was not a brilliant approach.

They don't call them shifts for nothing. On air schedules were changed like socks. Chris Morgan worked the evening hours but everyone else seemed to be playing golden oldie musical chairs. Harry and I had fun working together in the afternoon and Red was going strong at home and away.

The afternoon shift is like a vacation compared to the frantic activity on the early morning show and the need to roll out of bed about the same time the bars close. Afternoon Jocks can sleep until noon if they desire and get off duty in time for happy hour.

In the early days of rock and roll when the Baby Boomers were pimply-faced teens, the real radio stars were the evening Jocks, dedicating songs to young lovers, hosting high school hops, courting the coveted 12-18 audience. As the boomers aged and television stole most of the evening audience, the emphasis shifted to the early morning shows. Modern radio pours the bulk of the operating budget, including salaries, into morning shows, running the evening hours and often even so-called afternoon drive as cheaply as possible with low paid announcers or automation. The AM stations still courting the aging baby boomers now emit one old age insurance or medical treatment commercial after another. We were still being paid to entertain regardless of our time slots, but that was then.

The fun atmosphere at WQXI remained in the halls and offices and I enjoyed popping jokes, swapping gossip and clowning around to entertain my friends and co-workers, especially the females. such as Carmella Gonzales and Cristy Allen. The women tend to laugh at DJ antics much quicker than other Jocks who view one another as rivals for attention. I was fortunate to be employed at a station where management allowed fun and games as long as it did not interfere with work.

SIXTEEN

Here, There and Everywhere

Red Neckerson was in demand for charity appearances and I seldom refused a request to emcee, make a motivational speech, do a standup routine or judge a contest. The only ones I turned down were humiliating or dangerous stunts such as being hit in the face with pies or baseballs, being dunked in a tank of icy water, sky diving, and riding an enraged bull in a rodeo. Of course these refusals led to accusations from those who stood to make a profit, that I was a poor sport, a selfish Prima Donna. Well, hand me my tiara.

For every paid appearance any personality acquires, there are several dozen appeals for non-paid gigs. Working without compensation for a worthy cause is fine, though sometimes the people who request a celebrity's services are themselves well paid. Many pleas come from commercial establishments that promise "good exposure, lots of publicity." Those folks I loved to remind that appearing before their sparse crowds hardly exposed me as much as my nationally syndicated features on hundreds of stations with a total listenership somewhere in the millions.

The J. Walter Thompson Agency recruited me to shoot Canadian national TV commercials for a weed killer. They flew me to Toronto two years in a row and gave me a big budget for wining and dining in a luxury hotel. Most of the money I pocketed and ate at McDonald's. It was a unique experience to pay for their biggest breakfast platter with an American ten dollar bill. The McClerk had to call the manager over to help figure out the rate of exchange. After a few minutes of head-scratching they gave me the breakfast and twelve dollars and a few cents in change. Such a McDeal.

I was paid well for doing the national commercials, but Canada took fifteen percent tax off the top, the agent who booked me for the work took another fifteen, the syndicator wanted fifty percent, and after I paid state and national taxes, well I was at least glad for the great deal at McDonald's.

I had to be up early, ready to go to work, dressed in my Red Neckerson attire, which happened to be a red baseball cap, old plaid shirt, faded jeans and scruffy cowboy boots. The doorman kept giving me distasteful looks as I stood near the entrance to the luxurious joint.

"Sir, are you a guest in the hotel," he inquired.

"Yes, I am."

"Are you waiting for someone?"

"Yep."

More nasty looks.

Finally a limousine pulled up and an attractive lady from the ad agency got out to greet me, and said something about the shooting schedule.

Suddenly the doorman was all smiles, hustling to open the limo door for me.

"Oh, you're an actor! Have a great day Sir."

Yeah, that's me, an actor.

I got plenty of acting practice that day and the next. If an agency books eight hours of studio time, by George they're going to use eight hours. We did forty seven takes of the first day's lone commercial. The second day I deliberately neglected to keep count. I also posed for print ads and recorded a couple of radio spots. Canada must have been nearly swallowed up by weeds.

Newspapers and magazines were writing about Red Neckerson. A writer in Jacksonville, Florida described the character as a Paul Harvey with hemorrhoids. Paul Harvey, hemorrhoids or not, even quoted me on his broadcast. A young lady assigned to do a story on Red for the Atlanta Journal/ Constitution's Sunday magazine followed me around for five days taking notes and asking questions, mostly of a negative nature.

Like all reporters, she approached the chore with a pre-conceived notion. She had already decided that I was some fabulously rich, highly educated owner of expensive horses, living on a large estate who was exploiting poor white trash. Some of those are matters of opinion but the part about being rich is definitely wrong. I leased the farm where we lived and the horses paid for themselves. I'm still working on that first million.

She tagged along as I shopped for a cheap, white outfit at K Mart that I wore in a mud wrestling match with Willis the Guard as a preliminary fight at a Joe Corley kick-boxing event. It was billed as the Redneck Championship and it culminated with me clad in my white suit and cowboy hat being knocked into the big container of mud as planned. It was the countrified version of getting down and dirty.

Virginia Gunn, my one-time secretary turned TV star who by then hosted PM Magazine in Atlanta did a feature on me as Red and a young lady in Chattanooga, Debbie Bear, star of Chattanooga's PM Magazine also interviewed me for her program. TBS had a program entitled Winners and they filmed a long Red Neckerson success story at my farm and at the radio station which ran on national television.

As a complete surprise, Red was heard coming over the radio in the Robert Duvall movie, Tender Mercies. If anyone was compensated it wasn't me. It's amazing how much national publicity a person can receive without making a nickel.

The Super Station, WTBS was airing the sports show Football Saturday, hosted by former WQXI News Director Bob Neal from the Atlanta Fulton County Stadium Club. It was a lighthearted show with Alex Hawkins, former Falcons coach Norm Van Brocklin and several other former pro athletes. I appeared on the show a few times as a typical couch potato, know- it-all fan. It was great fun and the most enjoyable TV I ever did. Ted Turner, owner of TBS allegedly canceled the show because he didn't like the gambling odds aspect. Like he never made a gamble.

Playing Red Neckerson on trips to other markets was generally an exhausting experience. Stations would bring me in as cheaply as they could with a plane ticket one notch above pet in a crate, book at least four or five commercial appearances in one day and bunk me in a seedy, trade-out deal motel. One marathon day in Johnson City, Tennessee had me running from one store or car dealer to the next all day long capped off with a midnight appearance at a bowling alley.

For two years in a row I flew by shabby commuter airlines to extreme upper Michigan for an all day emcee job at Iron Mountain radio's annual talent contest. This required me to ad lib between amateur bands for eight hours straight. My wife Dixie accompanied me on the second trip and we had fun despite learning in Chicago that the commuter airline for which we had tickets to Iron Mountain had gone out of business the day before. We had to buy tickets on another airline for which I was never reimbursed.

After the long day of broadcasting in a beer-soaked bar we were up early the next morning only to be greeted by a raging snow storm, something of a surprise to Atlantans in mid May. I kept telling myself, one of these days you need to type up a contract about payment, travel, food and accommodation expenses and exactly what you will and will not do while there.

I emceed a roaring, deafening, carbon monoxide producing tractor pulling contest following a day of store and car dealer remotes in Evansville, Indiana and was finally, mercifully driven to a motel where I mistakenly thought I could get some rest. A gang of drunken revelers slammed in and out of the room next to mine all night long, making it impossible to sleep.

Up before dawn in order to catch a plane home, I heard not a peep from my ratty motel neighbors. At last they had passed out and were trying to sleep it off. I turned the volume on the TV set up full blast, turned and pressed it against the paper thin wall separating our rooms and left.

Another memorable excursion was to Mobile, Alabama where former WQXI PD Bill Sherard was programming a station that carried Red Neckerson. I judged a grits eating contest at a shopping mall during the afternoon. An overzealous lady contestant grabbed her steaming bowl of grits and started gobbling them before they had a chance to cool a bit and suffered a seriously burned mouth. I presume she sued the station.

That evening I was to do a routine at a comedy club. Sherard assured me it would be no problem. The station had been hyping my appearance and there was a nice crowd. I had prepared fifteen to twenty minutes of material as usual because I thought that more than that is too much from one comic. The problem was with the owner. He told Sherard that Richard Pryor did forty-five minute sets and he wanted me to do two sets of that length. I seriously doubt that Richard Pryor was performing for the measly few hundred bucks I was getting.

I did ninety minutes that night, the last set consisted mostly of old commentaries that I read aloud while the audience talked among themselves, drank and ignored me while Sherard killed time next door at a nudie bar. I had learned previously that the commentary material as aired on radio did not go over especially well in standup comedy situations. Due to short attention spans mixed with booze, snappy one-liners are in order. Note to self: No more delays. Write that appearance contract.

Mike Dineen was program Director at a station in Columbia, South Carolina and they were airing the Neckerson commentaries. They booked me for an appearance at a shopping mall in the unpredictable month of March, and despite a forecast of snow and freezing rain Dineen talked me into getting on a flight to meet my throng of adoring fans. Actually, of all the crummy places to make an appearance, malls are in the top five. Someone from the station sets up a sound system, hangs station banners and hands over a microphone,and says, "Do about 20 minutes."

People do not go to malls to laugh. Most of the people who crowd around out of curiosity are old grandmothers with a gang of little grandchildren and the rest are teenagers who always greet radio personalities with insults and shouts of how they listen to the competition. If I tell a joke, they are heard to mumble, "I don't get it. Who is He? I never heard of him. What channel is he on?"

Dineen was employed at a hard rock, heavy metal type FM station, most likely not number one with the age 65-plus demographics.

As I launch into a commentary, some old lady will always walk right up and interrupt with, "What are you giving away?" What's free?"

My crowd of hecklers began to disperse rapidly as reports of a snowstorm spread and they headed for home. We had to stick around for a couple of hours to keep the sponsor happy.

Dineen managed to get me to the airport through the near blizzard where I learned that my flight to Atlanta was canceled. Big Deal. I'll catch the next one. There was no next one. I spent the night on a rock-hard chair in Columbia's small airport, tired, hungry and cold. The concession stands were all closed. Note to self; No more flights in March. At least Dineen wasn't bumming smokes.

Several times I was coerced into appearing at events in my boyhood hometown or surrounding area in Southern Illinois. WFIW in Fairfield aired my syndicated commentaries and they could also be heard on stations from St. Louis and Terre Haute, Indiana. I was a hit at Dixie's class reunion, a Fairfield Chamber of Commerce affair, an oil driller's banquet, a big Pork Producers festival and even at Rinard Hay Days.

Rinard is a few houses that were built close together by coincidence with a population of less than one hundred people. Commemorating the cutting and baling of hay is their only significant annual occurrence so they get together for a big picnic. As a teenager I had made a few bucks by helping to load bales of hay onto trucks and unload and stack them in oven-hot haylofts. It is nothing to celebrate. The Rinard old timers would repeat their standard routine whenever my name was mentioned;

"That Red Neckerson is Russell and Lena Curry's boy, Jerry."

Somehow the older generation always thought that both my names were being mispronounced as Gary and Corry, obviously due to my family's lack of proper enunciation.

"I used to hear him announcing them Southern Ella-noise football games sometimes, and he couldn't even per'nounce his own name."

"I cain't hardly believe that's him. I never heard him say two words when he was growing up."

They had a point. It was because after I said one word someone would yell at me to shut up.

There were several weekly publications that supposedly kept track of sales and additions of songs to station playlists along with glowing revues and records to watch. A programmer reading all of the so-called tip sheets and taking their advice would help record companies accomplish their goal, getting every release on the air, no matter how horrible. Fortunately, no one believed the hype. Almost all of the tip sheets sponsored annual conventions where radio personnel and record moguls gathered to throw marathon drinking parties.

I attended the Bobby Poe Convention, the Bill Gavin conventions and the Ron Brandon conventions all held in Atlanta and a few out of town. Major record companies all had hospitality suites where radio people could drink free and pick up copies of their latest records. The hospitality suites usually had bigger crowds than the seminars and panel discussions. Many of the attendees who actually mingled and networked were looking for job leads.

Organizers put me on a panel to talk about creating jokes and humorous promos, but there is not much one can say except to read, practice writing bits and try to relate to the audience. Over the years I have encountered a lot of people who became quite irritated assuming that I had some simple recipe for humor writing that I would not reveal to them. Well, actually my method was revealed in a Red Neckerson column as follows:

Quite frequently someone will express curiosity concerning the source of my creative and hilarious thoughts with a polite query such as "how do you come up with all that inane drivel?" Being of a modest nature, my normal reply is "Money." I feel it is time to confess. Most of the time, I say and write gibberish, I mean, humor, for free and I do have a formula that I am ready to reveal.

To become a successful, poverty-stricken writer of jokes, humor columns, commentaries and internet hoaxes, follow these instructions; Twist, exaggerate and embellish everyday events so that they appear to be ridiculously funny. In other words, lie a lot.

Do something really stupid, and then claim a neighbor, relative or friend did it and make fun of that person.

Invent some invisible playmates with funny names that you can quote. The easiest way to create a person without working up a sweat and spending a lot of money is to go through the phone book and pick two odd last names such as Forkner and Gutz and put them together. It is always a good idea to add a Q for the middle initial. For some reason that puzzles even us comic geniuses, Q's are funny. At least that's what my friend Forkner Q. Gutz claims, ha ha ha, excuse me. But beware, he lies a lot.

Pick on public figures when they get caught doing something that you managed to get away with.

Stop writing occasionally to take on more liquid. A dehydrated humorist can only create dry humor, which is lost on most people. If someone asks you how many drinks you have had, yell something funny like "Shut up, I'm working!"

Use a lot of time tested phrases such as, "What's up with that," AReminds me of the time," "Don't even go there," "You gotta' be kiddin'," and "Are you carrying any contraband?"

If stricken with writer's block, (clinical term: brain constipation) many thought provoking topics can be gleaned from public restroom walls, wallpaper and radio gardening shows.

Most important of all, when you hear a good bit, steal it.

That's it. My conscience is clear. This advice will not be repeated, so all aspiring humorists should memorize and save it along with their Best of Dear Abby columns.

Independent promoter Jimmy Davenport booked Red Neckerson as the entertainment for the awards dinner at a Bobby Poe convention in Washington. Red was on a lot of radio stations. There were a lot more stations that he wasn't being carried on, which made him competition to the majority of conventioneers. Add to the equation that radio personalities are the worst audience in the universe because they resent anyone but themselves in the spotlight and you can deduce how my routine went over. They didn't boo. They just ignored me as I rambled on for twenty minutes or so. It didn't break my heart as I had witnessed other alleged Comics bomb just as badly at radio gatherings.

As record pluggers Long John, Billy Lemons, Bob Alou and Jimmy, "Otis T. Bear" Davenport and I waited at the airport to catch the hangover flight back to Atlanta, we picked up some reading material at a concession. While the rest of us chose magazines, Otis bought a big pharmaceutical book that listed all prescription drugs from A to Z. Flight security was more relaxed back then to say the least. When we boarded the plane, Otis made a left turn to the open cockpit door, handed the big book to the pilot and said, "Look in here and see if you can find what drugs we took last night."

Some of us will agree to do anything as long as it is far enough in the future. That is why I still make an occasional luncheon or after dinner speech, aka comedy routine. I book these appearances confidentially recalling the sense of fulfillment gained through making people laugh, the satisfying praise and appreciative handshakes after the speech, but then as the date approaches and it is time to gather the material. I'm seized with paranoia recalling past disasters.

I agreed to entertain at a Christmas dinner for a group of hospital workers from a north Georgia community. It was as usual, an un-paid appearance that I agreed to make after being assured that the medical staff was a fun-loving group of partiers. The event was held in a booze-free school cafeteria. I was introduced by a self-ordained Hell and damnation preacher following his frightening, marathon tirade. It was not an ideal warm up act for a comedian. His intro went something like this:

"And now, in this season when we celebrate the birth of Jesus Christ who suffered and died for us on the cross, here is someone calling himself... Red Neckerson."

The intimidated crowd sat silently as I ranted and raved with my best material about rip-off commercialism, gaudy decorations, greedy kids, and obnoxious shopping crowds. My wife was the only sole who dared to laugh. I cut the routine short and the dour man of the cloth launched into another sermonette about infidels who would defile the most holy, wonderful and glorious season of all. We fled as the choir struck up a rousing bluegrass rendition of Handel's Messiah. I wanted to escape quickly fearing that they were about to bring out the snakes.

Another time I was hired to provide a good dose of Southern humor at a convention for pharmacists. At least it was a paid gig. I had learned that anytime a person donates his services or works for a pittance his efforts are perceived as having little or no value and he is treated with disdain.

The group of surly, Northeastern liberal pill counters apparently had all of their worst suspicions about the South conformed as I struggled through 30 minutes of sneers. I wanted to bail out after a few minutes but when one is booked to do a half-hour, there's nowhere to run, no place to hide. I finally closed by asking who passed out the Quaaludes.

Somewhat shaken and resentful I left the place realizing I had another appearance booked for the following evening in Illinois, 500 miles away with no time to write new material. The same speech brought gales of laughter and applause from a group of small businessmen. Go figure. My advice on public speaking and comedy: Don't follow a fundamental preacher, don't try redneck material on a redneck audience and Yankee pharmacists are good for practice.

SEVENTEEN

What a Crowd! What? A Crowd?

In the course of a lifetime we meet and become acquainted with a lot of people. I believe all were sent to us and us to them for a purpose. I have been blessed beyond measure with those I have known and shared life experiences with. My greatest friend after Dixie was Mike Clark whom I first met when he was a record promoter and I was a Program Director. He was the most versatile talent I have ever known as a musician, builder, technician, computer expert, photographer, music producer and authority on collectibles including classic cars. With all his abilities he was modest and humble, even shy until someone tried to take advantage of him. They never tried it more than once.

Mike worked for Bill Lowery's company, eventually acquiring a half interest in the Southern Tracks recording studio, and finally gaining full ownership when Bill passed away. Many big artists still record at Southern Tracks including Bruce Springsteen. Mike's studio ranks as one of the best in the nation. Mike and I shared a love of country life and horses far from the traffic and pandemonium of the music and radio business. Mike and his wife Melissa first met at our farm and the four of us shared countless happy times.

At the height of Red Neckerson's popularity Mike suggested that we produce a comedy album and naturally I was agreeable. We would invite our friends in the music and radio fields to an evening of fun in the recording studio and roll the tape while I pontificated. Bill Lowery, the most positive person on earth, was always eager to host a party and the large room was packed with imbibing Neckerson fans and a few toleraters.

Mike thought we should record at least forty-five minutes of material then edit it to about thirty minutes of the best stuff. Bill Lowery gave me a rousing introduction and I started orating while the audience continued drinking and talking louder, often yelling and whistling in order to make sure they would be heard on the record. One woman brought a police whistle.

I ran out of breath after about twenty minutes of shouting over the loud-mouthed drunks and called for a break. Jim Davenport, aka Otis T. Bear, took the opportunity to perform his notorious toilet paper routine. He had a habit of stripping totally nude from the waist down whenever a good-sized crowd gathered, sticking one end of a twenty foot long strip of toilet paper in his butt crack, lighting the other end and casually strolling through the mob as he were merely stretching his legs. As they like to say in TV newscasts, "But then, something went terribly wrong."

Otis had performed the stunt enough times to know exactly when to pull the plug, so to speak, to avoid being burned. However, CBS Records promotion man Don Miller whipped out a cigarette lighter as Otis ambled down the aisle and lit the paper a few feet from the naked posterior. We were all treated to the odor of singed hair and a painful yelp from Otis as he frantically groped and snatched to rid himself of his comedy material. It was a tough act to follow and laughter was noticeably less in my second session with many of the woozy audience walking out. It was a great party. Great recording session, not so much.

Mike Clark, production ace Harry Schuster and I were in Southern Tracks studio a few nights later trying to edit the tape into something coherent to no avail. Our friend John Long and Mike had made a stab at salvaging the master tape earlier but there was no way to eliminate the loudmouthed interference from the well-lubricated audience. As if we didn't have enough aggravation, singer/songwriter Joe South stumbled in around midnight, shivering from the cold and tried to wheedle Harry or I out of a winter coat. Don't it make you want to go home?

Take two, they're small. Mike and I decided to pare down the material, gather a small crowd of friends, relatives and co-workers who at least claimed to be sober for an afternoon recording session. It went amazingly well compared to the first attempt, and in less than an hour we had a tape that was able to be pressed into a vinyl disc with minimal editing.

I designed the jacket and titled it "Jist Ask Yerself," a recurring Red Neckerson phrase. The LP sold a few thousand copies around Atlanta and was nominated for a Grammy in the spoken word category. It was the hottest album since Willis Caswell and the Crimson Cowboys. Big whoops. Maybe if we had given Joe South a coat he would have told us how to sell a million copies.

Another note to self: If they can get your act free by turning on a radio they are not likely to buy it on a recording.

Mouthing the syndicated commentaries was a wonderful outlet for venting frustrations while utilizing my genetic comedic traits. I found it easy to take anything that irked me and turn it into a humorous tirade. Occasionally I noticed some folks clammed up in my presence in fear of ending up as commentary material. A lot of them did.

Many times an interviewer or a friendly but curious soul will ask which commentary is my all-time favorite. I don't have one. I don't even remember the vast majority of them because they number in the thousands.

Perhaps some people have more favorite things than I do, since I have no favorite song, movie, color, food, TV show or movie star. Maybe I'm just fickle because my preferences are always subject to change but I prefer to call myself open-minded. Admitting to someone that you have a favorite usually causes a sneer since it always differs from their favorite. I like all my commentaries or I wouldn't have done them. It is satisfying when someone tells me how much he enjoyed a certain bit he heard years earlier on a station a thousand miles away. It makes me realize how far I have come from being a shy kid in Rinard, Illinois.

Ch, Ch, Ch Changes

Unless radio station employees are extremely naive, and some are, major changes seldom come as a surprise. Once supervisors start avoiding contact, no criticism or encouragement comes from programming and a general air of paranoia permeates the joint, it is time to quickly compile resumes and audition tapes. When Assistant PD Kelly McCoy resigned to accept a job at WSB FM, some folks suspected he knew something. A seeming lack of interest from management, hush-hush meetings behind closed doors and engineers being overheard mumbling about automation equipment did nothing to encourage feelings of security. J.J., Harry and I joked on the air about the coming automation. We may as well go out laughing.

Some deep thinker in management came up with the theory that since no one seemed to care that MTV was automated, they wouldn't mind listening to an automated radio station. Despite the fact that MTV did indeed employ Video Jocks and comparing TV to radio made as much sense as comparing movies to badminton, the theory was accepted as rational contemplation. This was before the continuous playing of music videos on MTV bombed and their programming was replaced with creepy reality shows featuring foul-mouthed, sex-mad teenagers. That might have been a more intelligent format for WQXI.

At least automation was a cost-cutting measure. No one could argue with that. The "We don't need no stinkin' DJs" approach was a disaster and soon the company was leasing out blocks of airtime to anyone who could pay a few hundred bucks a week. Eventually, a company leased the facility full-time and turned it into a full-time sports talk station. I have been a lifelong sports fan, therefore I would never listen to their inane gibberish and allow them to ruin it for me.

As Red Neckerson noticed, "More music and less talk" on AM radio has been replaced with "No music and all talk." Some stations that have already worn out the previously reliable topics of politics, racism and sex have resorted to 24-hour a day sports chatter. The programming is basically a perpetual pre-game show. My cousin, Sy Gogglin tuned in to a sports talk station last week and waited 3 days for a game to start.

Talk stations have dominated the old, worn out, staticy AM band for years and now the virus has started to spread to FM, once the domain of listener-free classical music broadcasts and long-haired, drug addled hippies whispering reverently while introducing Devil worship music as a counter balance to the screaming, cornball Jocks spinning bubblegum on AM.

Gullible audience members, most of them inebriated, phone in their unreasoned opinions thereby becoming unpaid employees of the cheapskate station owners. We may rest assured that no stations will be migrating to Mexico in search of cheap labor.

As I finished an afternoon air shift I was paged over the intercom and asked to report to the General Manager's office, thus alerting every soul in the building that I was being fired. A few of them angrily offered suggestions to tell management where to go and what to kiss. Since I had advised my friend Harry, who was also being sacked, that no one would recall our first day on the job but everyone would remember our last day, we should exit with class and dignity. I actually doubt if anyone remembers either day, but it sounded good at the time and we strolled out clutching our severance checks and headed to the nearest bar. We tried to drink up our checks but couldn't.

The first item on my to-do list was to purchase and install equipment for a home recording studio in order to keep the Red Neckerson syndication in operation. Harry helped me with that project as I never bothered to absorb any electronic knowledge beyond "press here for on, here for off."

For a year or so I played with the horses and enjoyed time with my family. Either 20 or 25 new commentaries had to be written, recorded and mailed to the duplicating company each month depending on the broadcast calendar. It was not easy squeezing 25 commentaries onto a 30 minute tape. I jotted down notes and ideas on current topics, fads and irritants then sat down and typed up the month's worth of wit and wisdom in one or two sittings. I have mastered the art of procrastination. I'll explain later if I get around to it.

EIGHTEEN

If You've Got The Money,
I've Got The Time

After a while I missed the camaraderie and action of a regular radio job. Harry and I decided to check with the people at WYAY, a Country music outlet then known as Y-106 FM. Harry had been making a living doing voice-over work but we were both ready to get back into the fast lane. We scheduled an appointment with Y-106 Operations Manager, Bob Neil, not to be confused with Bob Neal the sportscaster. I was hired to join the station in my Red Neckerson character. My commentaries would be sold to sponsors and I would be compensated with a percentage of the sales. What could go wrong? Harry received no offer but soon landed a job as Producer of the Randy Miller morning show at Z-93.

I started work the following Monday morning with The Zoo Crew, anchored by Rhubarb Jones. After 9 o'clock when the office personnel were going about their daily chores, I wandered up the hall and inquired where to find Bob Neil. I was told that he was no longer with the company. About a day after hiring me and before I started, he had accepted a job at WSB and left the station. What the heck is it with my first day on the job bombshells? For a while there I thought this may be an even shorter-lived gig than my week at WIBV. Fortunately, General Manager Bob Green was quite pleased to add Red Neckerson to the Y-106 stable and I had another home away from home.

The station was playing a mix of Country and certain pop hits. They had a strong staff of DJs from the Morning Zoo Crew with Rhubarb Jones, the bubbly Dixie Lee from nine to noon, then a smooth, affable afternoon personality George Mason Dixon, a bombastic Johnny "Stonewall" Jackson and night shift pro John Roach.

Bill Dollar later joined the station as a DJ and he tells of a practical joke one of the engineers, Sandy Griffin played on George Mason Dixon. He switched the receiver from Y-106 to a hard rock station and that is what boomed through the studio monitors and George's headphones instead of the Country song he was actually playing. When George ran back to find an engineer, the guy would switch it back, mosey into the control room to listen and say "Sounds fine to me." He would then leave the control room and go turn it back to the rock station. This went on about four times before George figured out he was being punked when the engineer blew it by giggling like a little girl.

George happened to be on the air January 28, 1986 when a bulletin from the news department interrupted his show. The space shuttle Challenger had exploded upon launching killing all seven crew members. George, a solid professional and one of the least offensive DJs in the business started the previously programmed song without comment and realized too late that it was an unfortunate selection as Kenny Rogers belted out the opening phrase, "Let's go out in a blaze of glory." Some listeners accused him of deliberately making fun of the disaster and others deemed it a poor attempt at a tribute to the lost crew. In reality it was only a weird coincidence.

Ron Hudspeth had been a long time columnist for The Atlanta Journal-Constitution newspapers before leaving to publish his own monthly entertainment news magazine. Ron and I had crossed paths several times at celebrity roasts, radio station promotions and in Buckhead bars to become casual friends. Shortly after I joined Y-106 he recruited me to submit a monthly humor column. I jumped at the chance and enjoyed being a published columnist for nearly twenty years. It was written under the Red Neckerson byline but I had learned much earlier that the countrified, ungrammatical lingo utilized in the spoken commentaries did not translate well into print. I wrote the columns with the same formula used to hammer out the monthly stack of radio commentaries; wait until the deadline and finally start writing.

The Y-106 Morning Zoo Crew was a team effort consisting of News Director Bob Glascoff, a young lady by the name of B. J. Williams who was the hardest working newscaster, Public Service Director and personality I ever encountered, DJ, Program Director and board operator "Commander" Dave Foster, and the star of the show, Warren "Rhubarb" Jones, arguably the best Country music Disc Jockey in America.

Extras in the cast included Jim Basile the traffic reporter, and for a while Paul Ossmann, WXIA TV meteorologist. My routine was to grab the morning newspaper and hack out a couple of commentaries on a hot topic. Rhubarb called on me frequently to join in the show with ad lib jokes and observations.

All You Need Is Love?

Since the lone consistency in radio is change, account executives came and went along with sponsorships of my commentaries. When a couple of sales people who were good at marketing Red Neckerson left the station I could have made more money picking peaches, but hey, why does it always have to be about money? Oh, right. Food, gasoline, power bills, and such small luxuries always come in handy. .

Program Directors come and go, which is usually a good thing, and Herb Crowe had been hired to relieve Dave Foster who remained on the air with Rhubarb, then remained seated for his own show from 10 A.M. until noon, until Bill Wise took over as PD and fired Foster.I reminded Mr. Crowe that without a sponsor I was working for nothing and I would be leaving at the end of the month unless I was put on the payroll.

Management agreed to pay a salary and named me morning show Producer, which actually meant that I would be writing material for the Zoo Crew in addition to creating my daily commentaries. Since I was not handing taped cartridges to the Jocks, running for coffee and booking obscure guests on the show, Dan Blankowski was eventually hired as Producer.

My work day began between 5:00 and 5:30 A.M. by grabbing the newspaper and banging out a page of one-liners on a manual typewriter. I would then conjure up a few short routines for character voices that could be taped or phoned in My job was to come up with at least 4 or 5 pages of current comedy each morning. I had been doing the same thing off and on for decades so it was not impossible.

The Zoo Crew regulars, Rhubarb, Dave, Bob Glascoff, B.J. Williams and I met after each show to swap ideas for new comedy bits to be aired the following day. A young part-time DJ and van driver, Eric Lanford joined the cast with zany impressions of celebrities. In addition, the company owned a syndicated service called The American Comedy Network which supplied several features each week. We would review the material and decide which bits to use if any. We were never at a loss for material and there was some sort of entertainment in every stop set.

Rhubarb was a glib personality and could be quite funny or serious depending on the situation. He is also one of the rare DJs who don't mind crediting the writers. Most insecure types want the audience to believe they are ad libbing all their funnies.

Rhubarb Jones is widely known for his charity endeavors such as the Rhubarb Jones Celebrity Golf Tournament held annually to benefit the Leukemia and Lymphoma Society. During my days as part of the Zoo Crew he spent the entire month of June each summer standing in the blistering heat of asphalt parking lots collecting pennies in his March Across Georgia for the same cause. People turned out in droves to meet him, lugging big jars full of saved pennies which were taken to the bank by the millions.

A lot of additional cash was raised in paper money and checks of course, and I recall one afternoon when Country artist and patriot Lee Greenwood pulled up, dropped three thousand bucks into the pot and was gone in a flash before anyone could make a big deal out of his generosity. Rhubarb has raised untold millions of dollars for charities including the Saint Jude Hospital for Children which benefitted from an annual on-air telethon that always amassed hundreds of thousands of dollars in pledges. I doubt if any one radio personality working in a single market has ever come close to matching Rhubarb Jones success as a fund raiser for worthy causes. I also know that he secretly aided many poor or down on their luck people.

Among his dozens of awards Rhubarb Jones is a past winner of Radio Personality of the Year from both the Country Music Association and the Academy of Country Music. He has been the recipient of the Disc Jockey of the Year award from Billboard Magazine and was voted one of the top Country Music Personalities of the Century by Radio and Records Magazine. He was inducted into the Country Music Hall of Fame in 2001and is a one of the initial inductees into the Georgia Radio Hall of Fame. Despite his credentials, popularity and value to the community in a penny-pinching move by Citadel Broadcasting, the current owners of WYAY, he was dismissed. At the beginning of his career, Rhubarb worked his way through college at a small market radio station in the same manner that I did and he went on to obtain a Master of Arts degree. He now teaches mass communications at Kennesaw State University.

In case you are still wondering, yes, most DJs are insecure and for good reason. I have witnessed station management insist that all Jocks sign contracts. This gave the more naive employees the false impression that their services were so valuable the station wanted to lock them in for at least a year. Shortly after inking the pact, as they used to say in show biz, the signer would be fired and then discover that the contract prevented him from going on the air in the same market for at least six months. I always refused to sign a contract and contrary to mumbled threats, I was not fired.

Something in Red

Atlanta magazine has an annual Best of Atlanta issue and I was named funniest radio personality, intentional division. As a swipe at Libertarian talk show host Neal Boortz, he was named funniest radio personality non-intentionally. Neal is so "unintentionally hilarious," he has since been syndicated nationally and is raking in money hand over fist. We should all be lucky enough to make millions of dollars accidentally.

I took my selection as an honor since I believed it to be accurate, and I'm sure Rhubarb Jones recommended me for the title. I was instructed to pose on a bright red couch in all white formal attire topped with my red baseball cap for a lovely glamour shot that was published in the magazine. I suppose that is a fish halfway out of water situation.

Another time I was required to wear a tuxedo was when I emceed a concert by the Cincinnati Symphony that featured the music of The Beatles. It was either me in a tux or Yoko who caused the Beatles to break up. I've always had a problem equating ultra-classy affairs with rented clothes. I can't help but wonder who last wore the monkey suit.

The most satisfying honor bestowed upon me during my days at Y-106 was when the staff voted me King of the winter carnival, a fancy, PC phrase for our annual office Christmas party. The vote winning Queen was Alison Reardon, Administrative Assistant to the General Manager. Alison later started filling in part time on the air, using the name Alison West. She was soon promoted to full-time evening DJ before leaving for opportunities in other markets. She has shared the Country Music Association's Personality of the Year award four times as one half of the Andy and Alison show on WIVK FM in Knoxville, Tennessee. I had the honor of working with both the best male Country music personality in America, Rhubarb Jones, and the best female Country music Disc Jockey, Alison West. I even danced with one of them.

Don't Be Nervous, Don't Be Rocky, You're Our Guest Country Disc Jockey Now

On the outside listening in, playing songs and making occasional comments seems simple enough. Someone in charge thought it would be a swell idea to select volunteers from the audience to record guest Disc Jockey programs to be aired on Sunday evenings.

Though I was never allowed to do a single DJ show using my real name, not that I had any desire to do so, I was saddled with the chore of recording amateur Country Jock wannabes, prompting and prodding them through a couple of hours in my Red Neckerson persona and doing most of the talking. No matter that it was forcing me to go totally out of character again. Listeners mailed letters begging for a chance to be the guest DJ, declaring that they would be wildly hilarious personalities.

Once they arrived at the studios for their scheduled taping sessions, they were nervous and inhibited almost to the point of panic. After the first session or two we typed up several stock phrases and generalities on cards for them to read instead of sitting mute, afraid to speak. We left blank spaces where they were to insert their names; "This is_____ on Y-106 FM." Often it would come out, "Mumble mumble, This is.........uh......Y106 FM." At this point I would stop the tape and yell, "Try to remember your name!" This of course would intimidate them further and cause them to become even more clammed up. Thankfully, B.J. Williams was usually assisting in the taping sessions and I could walk out and leave it to her. She and I were usually the only members of the air staff who were not terrified of a little extra work. After a few weeks not many people showed interest in becoming a guest DJ and we were down to recruiting relatives and friends, most of whom were no better than the once eager volunteers. Mercifully, the guest DJ gimmick was canceled. Becoming an on-air personality is not something anyone can do without training. A pro just makes it sound easy.

You Never Even Called Me by My Name

Bill Wise followed Herb Crowe as Program Director. After a while he was called Operations Director and eventually became General Manager. His famous quote was, "You can't win on the 9th floor." This meant, "Run yourselves to death night and day making non-paid public appearances.for my benefit."

Gary Lee Corry's name was never uttered on Y-106 or Y-104 but Red Neckerson was over used to the point of burn out. I also filled in as a newscaster for days at a time under the name of Gary Russell. Anyone who didn't recognize the voice as Red Neckerson must have damaged their hearing by listening to Led Zeppelin.

Why the paranoia over the well-established Corry name in the market was not explained and I was never curious enough to inquire. Obviously the resume as a major market morning personality and Program Director made someone uncomfortable. At least I didn't have to sign anything using my real name.

Bill Wise decided we should have family style picnics where the listeners could meet and greet the staff, receive autographed photos, enjoy free hot dogs and soft drinks and listen to live bands. The Zoo Crew made pitches on air for stores or companies to donate the hot dogs, buns and drinks for mentions. Local bands were invited to play for the publicity. I thought it was humiliating and a no-class move for the station. If we couldn't afford a couple hundred bucks worth of hot dogs I would not have held a picnic.

Big crowds turned out for these early evening gatherings since the magic word was "free," and we sat at tables autographing our mug shots by the hundreds. Most of the so-called fans standing in line were small kids who had no idea who we were, but it was fun to imagine, "If I was a major league baseball player charging for these, I'd be a lot happier."

For the first time in my life I learned about writer's cramp. Most people were nice and polite, but as always a few were obnoxious. Some dictated long, embarrassing or lewd phrases they wanted the DJ to dedicate to someone, others mumbled, causing their names to be misspelled or they had a weird way of spelling a common name, only telling the signer after they had ruined a photo. At the end of the day it was not real uplifting to notice your autographed pictures littering the grounds, thrown into trash cans and lying in the restroom urinals.

Without fail, anytime a radio personality appears in public at least one disgruntled soul will make it a point to say they have never heard of you and have never listened to your station. Management instructs DJs to smile sweetly and try to win them over by inviting them to listen. I never sunk that low. They would not have been pleased to learn how I replied to such critics, but it was similar to the way I responded to nasty phone calls. If they complained to management I lied, denying I said those awful words.

The personalities were each scheduled to drive the company van on prize patrols one day a week during the noon hour, calling in reports and giving away T shirts, caps and other trinkets. I thought it quite foolhardy for us to announce that our female newscaster, B. J. Williams would be at a certain location alone, vulnerable to any sick pervert in the listening audience so I accompanied her on assigned drives.

Male radio personalities have enough problems with mentally deranged listeners who think the DJ or news person is speaking only to them and conveying secret messages. An unescorted woman asking such weirdoes to come meet her is a design for disaster.

Most of the time hardly anyone took time out in the middle of the day to join us. Shortly after a few sales people started selling the so-called prize patrols and demanding that we go hang out for at least an hour in some far flung locale, I refused to do any more non-paid prize patrols.

Among the sales staff, which incidentally took pride in announcing that they never listened to the Country music station they are supposed to be selling, a personality who refuses to work free so the sales type can collect large commissions is accused of having a negative attitude.

The most popular emcee job was introducing major Country acts at Lanierland, the outdoor music park and arena north of Atlanta. There was a large dining room and a screened-in porch backstage where delicious home cooked meals were served to the performers and radio people. Most artists mingled and chatted with the DJ as they enjoyed the food. Having come from a rock and roll background, I was pleasantly surprised at the reception the audiences always gave to the emcees. Rock concert crowds of mostly rowdy young people tend to be somewhat hostile to anyone on stage except the artists they have come to ogle while they have their hearing destroyed. The venue was co-owned by Tommy Bagwell and the Jones family, Robert, Leon and his wife Brenda, and their daughter Cindy Mills. The grand matriarch of the family, Mama Lois, cooked the delectable feasts with love and urged everyone to eat a healthy meal as if she were their own sweet grandma. The warm, friendly family always made the DJs and artists feel welcome and appreciated. They also paid us. The park sadly closed in 2006 after a 36 year run.

Goin' Down South

Y-106 was originally licensed to the city of Gainesville, north of Atlanta and had a strong signal everywhere except south of town. The company made a bold move by purchasing a station southwest of Atlanta, changing the call letters to WYAI and launching the simulcast Y-106 and Y-104 FM. It was the first time that the same programming was aired on two FM frequencies in the same market.

Theoretically, this gave the stations access to many thousands of new listeners in the southern reaches of the survey area and would greatly enhance the ratings. In reality, the results were minimal. People who listened on the 104.1 frequency reported that they were listening to Y-106, the well established name.

The personalities were dispatched to various locations south of Atlanta handing out T-shirts, caps, donated hot dogs and soft drinks in an effort to woo listeners to Y-104. The public seemed to be slow catching on to a station calling itself by two names, Y-106 and Y104 FM. The plan for big ratings on Y-104 was a bust but not too disheartening to the owners of the company because the frequency was basically acquired as an investment. Within five years both stations were sold, WYAY to the Disney chain and WYAI to Cox Broadcasting, leaving most of the staff unemployed.

For well over a year Y-106 and Y104 achieved unprecedented ratings, winning the Country music battle with WKHX, known as Kicks, and becoming number one in the entire North Georgia survey area. Garth Brooks and the ensuing new Country artist boom at that time worked to our advantage over other formats. Young people were suddenly becoming Country music fans.

Most of the staff would gather waiting for the initial results of the ratings to arrive and when we beat Kicks again, GM Bob Greene would close down the offices and let the celebration begin. Barefoot soccer games broke out in the halls of the building. Our athletic and attractive Promotion Director Kim O'Shields would perform cartwheels and the splits while the cocktails and beer flowed freely. At least that's what they tell me. By the time the results came in I was usually at home taking a nap.

Our work both on and off the air had paid off, but of course it was never enough to satisfy management. When something succeeds in radio, they begin dreaming and scheming of ways to make it even better, usually by deleting whatever made them successful.

Bill Wise conducted a lunch time meeting with Rhubarb, Steve Mitchell, B.J. Williams and me at a nearby restaurant and took the opportunity to chew us out for failing to dress, in his words, like NASCAR drivers.

He actually wanted us to plaster call letters all over our clothing and venture out in public like walking billboards. We already wore blue jackets adorned with garish bright yellow and orange call letters and our names in cool weather but he deemed that insufficient promotion. I was tired and irritable as usual after a long morning of writing several pages of comedy material. I walked out on the meeting thankful that he hadn't as yet insisted that we have the call letters tattooed on our foreheads.

He'll Have to Go

After coercing Red Neckerson into taping guest DJ shows, making serious, heart-felt pleas for charities, emcee all sorts of upscale events inappropriate for a redneck character and everything totally out of place for the personality that was a nationwide success, programming savants deduced that they could recruit new listeners by the tens of thousands while retaining all of our Country music fans by pretending to be sophisticated.

Red Neckerson commentaries were taken off the air. I announced that I would be leaving since that meant no more paid appearances and Bill Wise, who was General Manager by then but continued to act as Program Director, told me I could continue to emcee, do remote broadcasts and everything but daily commentaries. Perhaps that seemed logical to someone. I remained as a writer and occasional guest on the morning show. I was on stations scattered all across the country but not on the air regularly where I was employed.

We stopped playing music by established Country artists in favor of the so-called hot, new cowboy hat wearers and took any Southern or countrified promos and jingles off the air as if this would have listeners flooding over from pop music stations.

News was down-played drastically and Bob Glascoff was fired. Eventually B.J. Williams also left after her salary and hours were reduced when she returned from maternal leave. B.J. was an important part of the Morning Zoo Crew in addition to being a tireless worker in public affairs and a proficient newscaster. The wheels were coming off the wagon as management seemed to be concentrating on nothing but the bottom line and salary deletions.

Popular midday personality Dixie Lee left, then evening Love Songs DJ Alison West. Rhubarb still anchored the morning show while his partners came and went, from Dave Foster to Johnny, "Stonewall" Jackson, to Kelli Roberts to Steve Mitchell. A good all night DJ, John Roach was soon to leave.

Bill Wise fired morning show producer Dan Blankowski and Production Director John Long. I had recommended John for the production job when the opening came up. We had been friends for years and he was the first person to recognize the potential syndication of Red Neckerson commentaries. He was an experienced programmer, air personality and a creative producer of commercials and promos which made him a target for underhanded politics leading to his termination.

Several office personnel were also fired and station morale was at rock bottom. Ratings increased nicely. Unfortunately it was for the wrong station as no new Yuppies tuned in to the Y stations and lots of Country music fans went over to Kicks.

Co-owner of the company, Dick Ferguson came to town from headquarters in Connecticut and interviewed staff members one at a time. As a result, Bill Wise was dismissed and Sales Manager Sally Appel was named General Manager. My duties had evolved into writing and recording commercials all day long while battling with the sales staff over missing copy, ignored deadlines and general lack of cooperation.

Account Executives, as they preferred to be called, are obviously too important to be bothered with details. They are notorious for tossing the production person a couple of scribbled lines and requesting at least two 60 second commercials be written. It's often either far too little information or far too much to fit into a 30 second or 60 second commercial. For a creative and irreverent soul, recording sales pitches is a rather mundane occupation but I kept getting in my licks through my humor column and the syndicated commentaries.

Arriving at work one morning about 5:15, I noticed a rather nasty memo taped to the control room door. Not being in my usual sunshine, lollipops and rainbows mood at that time of day, I struck a match to it. Extremely loud sirens started blaring and all the air was whooshed out of the control room leaving John Roach, the DJ on duty, breathless and rather surprised.

Security guards rushed in yelling into walkie talkies, scurrying around searching for flames. Calls were made to 911 and the fire department. Someone managed to stifle the alarm just before the sprinkler system was to kick on flooding the entire floor. "An accident," I claimed. My most serious offense was waking the security guards before breakfast.

For several months Y-106 and Y-104 managed to compete despite our whittled down staff. Morale was vastly improved with Sally Appel at the helm but she did not enjoy being the GM and announced her resignation. We were assured by the owners that a new GM would be soon be hired. Finally Dick Ferguson notified us that he was coming to town with a big announcement. Of course speculation ran rampant and as we assembled in the conference room, some of our amateur comedians started writing ridiculous names of the top ten candidates most likely to be named the new General Manager. They were only funny for a few minutes.

Mr. Ferguson announced to a totally shocked gathering that the stations had been sold to the Disney Corporation, owners of our main competitor

WKHX. They had grown frustrated with battling us for the Country music audience and decided to buy us out, spin off Y-104 and program Y-106 to the older Country listeners while maintaining the Kicks audience. Naturally, the sale meant that most of the Y station's support personnel and some members of the air staff would be fired. The day that had started off all fun and games ended like a bad dream.

The new owners would not need sales reps, engineers, and office workers. Since it would take a while for the sale to be approved by the FCC we kept the needle peaking while most people sought new jobs. The GM of Kicks, who introduced himself as the best there ever was, interviewed everyone individually and allowed them to make pitches to retain their jobs,. Most of those accepted agreed to large salary cuts. I never bothered to ask for a job with the company I had spent the last eight years trying my best to defeat. I had the Red Neckerson syndication to rely on for a living and I couldn't wait to grab a severance check and flee from the smug overlord.

One of the DJs, Bill Dollar, filmed all the members of the staff as they went about their daily chores and asked them to make comments and farewell speeches. I was recruited to narrate the film mimicking Walter Cronkite and it was played on a big screen at our farewell party. And that's the way it was.

NINETEEN

Runnin' On Empty

My radio career was winding down with only the syndicated commentaries going out monthly to a few stations. I despised the paperwork, billing and re-billing station owners who were rarely in the same city as my clients. Group ownership called for me to bill an office in Hoboken for my commentaries that were aired on a station in Possum Gulch and quite often they were totally unaware of the deal. Collecting got to be more time consuming and a bigger hassle than writing, recording and mailing the tapes. This was before MP3 files in my computer would have allowed me to send the award worthy and absolutely hilarious comments out with the click of a clicker thing. I'm still not especially computer savvy. When all the contracts with stations ended I stopped syndicating.

I was still writing columns for the Hudspeth Report and enjoying semi-retirement. Semi-retirement sounds like an old, worn out transport truck. Now that's appropriate. When you stop going in to work after several decades, you really love it at first. Life is just one long vacation. Then you get bored. Then you start liking the boredom. Some would call that laziness. I call it pacing myself.

My old friend Harry Schuster prompted me to work again at least a little bit, by recommending Red as a regular on Captain Herb Emory's Saturday afternoon NASCAR racing show on WSB AM. I didn't know a whole lot about automobile racing but it didn't seem to matter as long as my call-in reports were funny. For the next few years I popped wisecracks about the drivers, complicated rules and weird restrictions involved in the sport. Such a deal. All I had to do was sit here, monitor the show and when they broke for the first stop set, phone in my gut-busting comments and interact with Herb and his crew.

Most of the time it went smoothly, but once in a while, okay, it was frequently, someone would start calling our phone number and the call-waiting demon would cut off my words and screw up the report. I had forgotten that the wife and kids get approximately 56,000 phone calls a day. There is supposedly a way to disable the diabolical call waiting feature but my disabler must have been disabled.

Then there was the time the show ran after 9 PM and the kids were hosting a party. I dutifully racked my weary brain for some new material, wrote out my commentary and waited patiently for the cue to call in, only to hear faint, garbled voices and no dial tone. Some young genius had grown tired of annoying phone calls from other Cretins inquiring about the party. He threw the phone onto the roof of the garage without hanging up, making my phone inoperable. My screaming tirade shocked and spooked the keen teens so badly I ruined the party. For about 10 minutes.

The NASCAR experience inspired me to record a CD combining the best of the commentaries with new material. For some weird reason unknown to science, I tend to come up with my best material in pre-dawn hours. I would rise about 4 AM, sit at the kitchen table and write down the jokes. Finally feeling that I had exhausted about every angle I could wrestle into a funny routine while being confined to the lone topic of car racing, I resigned from the show to concentrate on writing. If anyone ever accuses you of being a wastrel, lounger, layabout, loafer, idler, do-nothing, slouch, laggard, lazy bum, or any combination thereof, just inform that judgmental name-caller that you are a writer. Writing often requires extended periods of deep concentration and rest which could give the false impression of indolence. Stick with your claim. Write those instructions down if you never write another word.

Been a Long Time Gone
Epilogue

Great programmers of music stations including Bill Drake, Kent Burkhart, Gordon Mc Clendon, Paul Drew, and several others believed a station not only had to be staffed by talented personalities but had to maintain an overall persona of its own. Consistency, every hour of everyday was the paramount goal so that a person tuning in at any time could immediately identify the station. Disc Jockeys were to entertain and adhere to format guidelines in speech and actions. Yeah, we're reminiscing. It's strictly past tense. It's all over now Baby Blue.

Sometime in the 80s big investors saw the great profits being raked in by successful radio stations and began petitioning congress to change the rules regarding ownership and service to the communities where stations were licensed. These investors had no clue that successful radio stations built their audiences with talented on-air people. Under the guise of free enterprise, large corporations were allowed to own as many stations as they cared to acquire as opposed to the old restrictions of no more than seven each AM and FM. Today the worst example is a company that owns over two thousand stations and runs them as cheaply as possible with profit their lone goal.

Tens of thousands of radio jobs have been lost due to syndication of entire programs and situations where one company owns most or all stations in a market. One skeleton staff is able to voice track and punch up computerized programming for several stations all located in the same building. Any time you hear a syndicated talker bragging about another station picking up his program, pause to think of the three or four people who have just lost their jobs. I'm glad that my syndicated effort was only a one-minute feature that cost no one his livelihood. In fact, I have motivated several plagiarists and imitators to make a good living.

There is little or no competition in many markets as station owners are allowed to buy out the competitors and change their formats as happened when the owners of WKHX bought Y-106/ Y-104. Exciting ratings battles and never-ending quests for one- up-man-ship between rivals is history.

Without competition it is inevitable that cheap, poor programming becomes the norm.

The Federal Communications Commission once demanded that a station must provide local service to the community of license but now that rule has been relaxed to near non-existence. There are no small and medium market training grounds for new Disc Jockeys to hone their craft and work their way up as was once required.

Over the past few decades upper management and programmers poured huge amounts of money into the coffers of researchers to give them the results they wanted. These experts in the use of mail-outs, phone surveys and focus groups gladly assured the big shots that listeners had no use for Disc Jockeys, local news or anything except non-stop music anytime past ten AM.

Research says, put a team show on in the mornings, have them snicker and giggle about sex, potty jokes and celebrity gossip then just keep the needle peaking as cheaply as possible the rest of the time. If it doesn't work, no prob. Hey, we did what the research said we should do.

Sadly there is no place for creativity or innovation. Radio is trying to out-Ipod commercial free Ipod, satellite and internet music outlets, a battle they are beginning to realize they have already lost.

Sixty years ago many were predicting that television would quickly sound the death knell for radio. On the contrary, radio wisely changed formats, leaving the adventure serials, soap operas, and variety shows to TV and thrived by playing recorded music introduced by personalities known as Disc Jockeys. Television did not kill radio broadcasting. It takes internet and satellite music programming to accomplish that and it will. Those huge radio towers will either be used for some other purpose such as cell phone bars or sold for scrap metal. I am thankful that I had the privilege and honor to help keep the needle peaking when radio was real.